Dedicated
to
my daughter Mischa

It Ain't Over 'Til...

An honest guide to navigating those make or break moments in business.

Jo Eckersley

Author - Jo Eckersley

Foreword;
Oli Barrett MBE

Contributors;
Laurence Fishman
- Partner at Nyman Libson Paul LLP Chartered Accountants
Emma-Jayne Broadway
- Founder & CEO, Talent Partnership Consulting
Caroline Hughes
- Commercial lawyer and Co-Founder of Hive Founders
David B Horne
- Author of Add then Multiply and Funded Female Founders
Mike Weston
 - Founder of Escape Velocity
Quinton McAffie
- Co-Founder of Social Places
Chris Worden
 - Founder of Director First
Jayne Lewis
- Leadership coach and Organisational Development practitioner
Warwick Hill
- Trusted adviser to over 200 startups

Contents

Foreword

By Oli Barrett MBE

There's a side of building a business that we still struggle to talk about. After meeting thousands of founders, I can tell you that it isn't their pitches, press releases or polished performances that stay with me. It's the quieter truth that every story is built on moments of doubt, difficulty and perseverance that are far less visible, but just as real.

One moment in particular has stayed with me. I was on a bus in San Francisco, heading back from an event. Beside me sat a founder who had just pitched on stage to thunderous applause. Their business looked unstoppable. But as we crawled through traffic, they turned to me and said, "We're going to run out of money in a couple of weeks." In an instant, a completely different conversation began.

We all know someone who has been involved with a business that didn't work out. We just might not realise that we know them. That is why this book matters.

I know this reality not just because I've heard these stories, but because I've lived them. When my first business fell apart, I didn't ask for help. I didn't talk about it - before, during or afterwards. I didn't share what I'd learned. I simply hoped no one would notice. Looking back, that silence made everything harder. It's one of the reasons I care so deeply about this book. Because back then, I didn't have it.

Jo Eckersley has written what so many founders - and the people who care about them - have needed for years: an honest, practical guide for the moments when things stop working and you don't know what to do next.

9

Not theory or sound-bites, but truth, tools and companionship from someone who's been there more than once and is still standing.

This book is for the founder who knows that there are times when it feels like you've run out of road. It's for the family member who wants to understand what's really going on. It's for the friend who senses something is wrong but doesn't know what to say. And it's for every supporter of entrepreneurship who believes we should celebrate resilience just as much as we celebrate success.

If that's you, read on. The stories and strategies in these pages may not remove the challenges, but they will help you face them with more clarity, more confidence, and the knowledge that you're not alone.

When things fall apart, it doesn't have to be the end of everything.

It can be the start of something better.

Introduction

Why We Need to Talk About Business Failure

The Unspoken Reality of Running a Small Business

Running a small business is often seen as the ultimate freedom - an escape from the 9-to-5, a chance to build something meaningful, to work for yourself, and on your own terms. It's a story many of us bought into, it's a story I have tried to write since I was 14 years old. The story hasn't gotten quieter for aspiring founders, it's sold in social media reels, startup podcasts, and glossy success stories. But behind the scenes, for many small business owners, the truth is far messier.

Because what few people talk about is how lonely, stressful, and fragile it can feel - especially when things start to go wrong.

This book exists because of that silence. Because of what's not said. Because of the shame and stigma that too often surrounds struggling in business. And because so many founders wait too long to ask for help - or don't even realise they need it until it's too late.

I am one of those founders. As a single mum of a challenging child (now a gorgeous young adult and mum in her own right) the only way I could manage to be there for my daughter, and generate an income was to work for myself, which fed neatly into my entrepreneurial approach to life anyway.

But five businesses in and lots of tough lessons later I am still astonished at how much support there is for founders to grow and scale, but how little help there is when things are really going pear shaped and you have no money to pay for advice to help fix things.

What This Book Is - and Isn't

So let's be clear: this is not a book about how to scale fast, hit 7 figures, or win investment.

There are plenty of books, incubators, accelerators and resources for that.

This is the book for when things really aren't going to plan. For when revenue dips, motivation flatlines, and pressure builds. For when you're facing really tough decisions and you don't know whether to push forward, pivot, or walk away. And very often that's exactly when there is no money to help solve the problems, or time to go on a business development course, learn about AI or learn sales 101. And let's face it the last place you want to be at that point is in a very public workshop surrounded by people whose businesses all **seem** to be doing so well.

So this is a survival guide for the harder moments of business ownership. It's the hints and tips, including how to use today's technology yourself, to help buy you and your business more time and space to think about the hard stuff.

It's also a recovery guide - for what happens during the chaos and after you hit the wall. For what happens when you realise it's not working. And for how you process, recover, and rebuild - mentally, emotionally, and financially.

Why We Don't Talk About Failure

We live in a culture obsessed with success. The stories we see and celebrate are the highlight reels: funding wins, snazzy new office launches, 'wish I'd thought of that' products, viral campaigns, revenue milestones. It seems like everyone is doing way better than you are, and you just need to catch up right?

We rarely hear about the flip side - the failed launches, the unpaid invoices, the silent weeks with no sales, the tax bills, those terrible sleepless nights. The fear that everything is moving at break neck pace and we can't keep up any more.

And because we don't talk about it, we assume we're the only ones going through it.
I know I did.

But the 2025 start up numbers tell a different story:

"In the UK, over 300,000 businesses close each year. That's nearly 1,000 every single day."

It's not so bad in the first year when an acceptable and probably expected 10% of businesses fail, but by the third year that figure rockets to over 70%. The most recent figures I could find with actual numbers showed that in 2023, the business birth rate was 11% (316,000 new businesses) and the death rate 10.8% (309,000 businesses closing). That's actually almost as many closing as opening.....

And these numbers are only escalating as technology makes it easier for anyone to build an app or a platform, or a business.

The true reality is that failure isn't rare. It's commonplace and becoming more so. It's not a reflection of your talent, drive, or worth. It's often the result of burnout, lack of cash flow, changing market conditions, personal circumstances - or simply timing.
And the more we normalise talking about it, the better chance we give founders to recover from it. And perhaps some of them won't end up closing their businesses at all.

What You'll Find in These Pages

This book walks you through the many faces of business struggle and potential collapse - from early warning signs to full wind-down.

It covers:

- Financial stress and the silent chaos of cash flow problems
- Customer disengagement and how to spot when the demand is disappearing
- Burnout and founder fatigue, and why it clouds decision-making
- Team dynamics, when culture turns toxic and leadership is questioned
- Compliance slip-ups, and how small legal oversights become big problems
- When technology can be your saviour and when it will trip you up
- How to manage stakeholders, investors and funders when you don't know what to say
- Debt, credit, and the emotional and logistical pressure they create
- The decision to close, and how to do it with clarity and confidence
- The recovery process, and how to begin again without shame

You'll also hear from my own experiences and other UK and International founders who've been there, who've come close to giving up, who've closed businesses, who've rebuilt.

Plus I've gathered useful insights for you from people I know and trust, who provide advice in these situations.

None of these stories are case studies in failure - they're all blueprints for resilience.

Who This Book Is For
This is for:
- The sole trader who's exhausted and barely covering costs
- The startup owner whose revenue has flatlined
- The entrepreneur wondering if it's time to call it a day
- The founder who is racing to keep up with change
- The dreamer trying to navigate a nightmare
- The business owner who needs to know it's not just them
- You, when you just don't know where to turn for help to turn things around

Whether you're in crisis, close to closing, or simply want to make sure your business doesn't drift into dangerous territory - this book is for you.

It's Not Over
The name of this book - It Ain't Over Til... - is a declaration. It's a reminder. Because whatever you're facing in your business right now, it doesn't have to define you.

There are steps you can take. There are people who can help. There is recovery on the other side - and in many cases, there's reinvention and relief, too.

But first, you need to see the warning signs. You need to understand what's really happening underneath the surface. You need to take a big, deep breath. And then decide what comes next.

This book is here to walk you through that process, and to walk alongside you -   step by step, with clarity, honesty and compassion, ideas and information.

"Closure isn't failure. Sometimes, it's leadership. Sometimes, it's wisdom. And sometimes, it's just the next right thing."

Why I wrote this book

I've come to realise that 'life is what WE make it'. Literally. We are actually completely in control, even though sometimes it really, really doesn't feel like it.

I first heard that phrase when an old man was walking past me as I was getting out of my car over 20 years ago and amongst his muttering, he said those exact words right next to me clear as a bell. I went in and wrote them down on the blackboard in my kitchen. Then beat myself up, took tough decisions, or applauded myself with them in rotation ever since.

The phrase underpins my bio, as everything I have done seems to lead to now and this book. Five businesses.....all closing for different reasons, not all bad, but still. Five. It's something I have spent most of my life embarrassed about, looking at it as a failure and more recently wondering how this qualifies me to advise anyone on anything.

But you see if I had carried on thinking like that I wouldn't have written this book, and shared my experience. Because in reality those businesses reflect a lot of learning. And a lot of success, as well as the challenge of living with their demise or watching them morph into something else that wasn't quite what I had intended.

It's certainly a lot of experience and insight I wish I'd had when I closed the first one. Well actually not exactly the first one - that was the school shop I opened when I was 14, and I don't think graduating from school I could actually have taken the shop with me.

But at 21 when I started working as a freelancer doing PR. That business grew fast and failed hard.

The next one left me the talk of the town for all the wrong reasons, divorced, bankrupt and very sad. Suicidal in fact.

But you know us entrepreneurs.

So on that freelance parade again, as a middle aged (infertile, so I'd been told) mum with a new baby (go figure). I tried to run businesses around pregnancy, childcare and very single parenting. Working from home helped me be 'present' for my child I thought.

Hmm...not exactly.

The problem was there was always a bigger business trying to get out. So I ran another agency, I split it in two. Then I thought I needed a tech co-founder (I actually didn't, I was just scared of what I didn't know back then). One fore-mentioned tech co-founder down, because building a saleable product was a whole different story to dabbling with R&D.

Long story. Not this one..

But five years, many tech partners later, a particularly nasty minority investor and Bang. It was over. Insolvent. Pre-Pack, packed up in someone else's suitcase.

And I just walked away.

To the incomprehension of everyone who knew me it seemed.

It looked like success. I'd got millions of pounds in investment for that business, no mean feat as a female founder (yes that is a real issue). I'd won InnovateUK funding, grants and a loan.

I had won national awards. UK Creative Screen Innovator of the Year. Female Tech Founder Computer Weekly Rising Star. The business and product even won International awards.

All before we launched the actual product.

Because for this business that was where it fell apart - we were always, almost, about to launch.

For five years and a pandemic.

When it crumbled and I gathered all those lessons up into numerous counselling sessions, I realised how It was hard to leave that part of my identity behind. But the truth, I have discovered, is you actually don't leave the successes behind. Those came with me, because they are fundamentally part of who I am, I made those successes happen.

The failures were me too of course, but they involved a lot of factors I sometimes had little control over. Because choice doesn't always equal control where you want it. Like female founder funding, sole founder challenges or just the sheer weariness of trying to do a lot as a single parent of both a business and a neurospicy child.

Facts: I walked away from my last business. I am happy.

And if this book saves one person from the mistakes, pain and loneliness I have been through over the years then all that will have been worth it. I incubated and accelerated. Thanked many mentors. Read hundreds of business books.

But in reality I wish I'd had THIS book.

I started again so you could have it.

Let's begin.

Chapter 1

The Cracks Before the Collapse - Early Warning Signs

The Myth

There is a prevailing myth that small business failure is sudden - a dramatic moment when everything caves in at once. I suppose it's a myth that's a little like its direct opposite, when we see overnight success, whether it's a pop star or a business, not realising the years of work that happened before the moment they shoot into our collective vision with all the trappings of super stardom.

But the hard reality is that business failure is not a sudden event. In most cases, it unfolds slowly - like a hairline crack from a tiny chip in a windowpane that spreads over time. Collapse doesn't come with a bang. More often, it begins really quietly as more of a whisper, a slow unraveling. If you look carefully you can see it takes shape gradually, built from missed signals, ignored discomfort, and the well-meaning denial that "it's just a rough patch." Founders often don't recognise they're heading towards the edge because the signs are quiet, familiar, frequently experienced even in a successful business, and easily dismissed.

This chapter is about those earliest moments - the subtle fractures that form long before a business falls apart. These moments rarely show up on a balance sheet. Instead, they reveal themselves in everyday behaviours, in small lapses of clarity, and in the quiet resignation that replaces energy and enthusiasm. We'll explore why these cracks are hard to see, how they disguise themselves as normal growing pains, and why recognising them early is the most powerful chance you have to recover and rebuild.

The Danger of Normalising Struggle

When you first start a business, discomfort is kinda expected. Late nights, unpaid invoices, stretching yourself thin - they all feel like part of the package. You assume that the long hours and stress are simply the compulsory tax you pay on ambition. You are probably working around other commitments, a family, a part time job, maybe even a full time role you hate but are scared to give up. You read about the founders who literally slept in their office and worked 24/7 to get their prototype built, you know you need to sacrifice now for the dream and the financial return that's coming later. But the danger lies in how quickly those temporary sacrifices become your normal operating mode.

Struggle becomes standard. Stress becomes routine. The hours of work and social life blend into a loop where you squeeze sleep into the small hours, as those get even more tiny. You stop noticing how hard things actually are because you've conditioned yourself to believe that "this is what entrepreneurship looks like."

Our current entrepreneurial ecosystem doesn't exactly help. Let's face it, struggling founders often also can't pay themselves what it costs them to live, aren't investable to our current unicorn driven investment ecosystem, and won't achieve those ever moving success based outcomes for a variety of reasons that all come along at once. You convince yourself that others are handling it better - that they're working through the same chaos and just not complaining. And let's not even go there with the pace of technology and the march of AI being so fast it can become a full time job just trying to keep up.

For many small business owners, this mindset takes hold quietly. You adapt to discomfort.

You become accustomed to chasing late payments, covering gaps with personal credit cards, skipping holidays, and living with that constant low-level hum of uncertainty and lack of sleep. It becomes normal to feel tired, worried, and stretched. So when the business genuinely starts to underperform, when the numbers no longer add up or the client list begins to shrink, it can be hard to differentiate a true red flag from the usual noise.

I was so used to chasing late payments, working weekends, and living invoice to invoice that I didn't realise my business wasn't actually sustainable. I was chasing the next investment, or commitment from a potential client, or trying to get a grant to help create some kind of cashflow to keep the team building a product that everyone seemed to want, (if we could just get it built and out the door).

And therein lies the risk - not just that things get worse, but that you might not realise just how much things have gone awry, until it's too late to shift course gently.

The Early Signs Are Often Emotional

Before the bank balance begins to falter, before the pipeline slows, before team members start to leave, the first place collapse shows up is inside the founder.

It starts with a sense of unease that you can't quite name. Perhaps it's a growing dread when opening your laptop. Perhaps it's a flatness during meetings where you once felt alive. Or maybe it's a quiet detachment from decisions you used to care about deeply.

That inner voice, the one that once buzzed with ideas and instinct, starts to go quiet - or worse, it starts to whisper doubts.

You feel it before you can explain it: the shift from drive to dread. A persistent, invisible pressure that tightens over time. It's not always dramatic. Sometimes it's just a nagging sense that something isn't quite right - yet nothing seems obviously wrong. Guilt was a big one for me. It wasn't just about the staff and their lives, or the investors and their money, or the prospective clients and the commitments we were making to them - I was sacrificing so much personally as a parent and in looking after myself, that I had to make sure this worked, I literally HAD to prove it would be a success, that I would be a success, and that was what kept me stuck in the loop.

What makes your gut instinct (or your mum as well in my case, who longed for me to get a 'real' job and reduce my stress), so hard to trust is that founders are conditioned to doubt their doubts. You're taught by the founder ecosystem to push through resistance, to keep going, to outwork discomfort. So when your gut starts speaking up, the temptation is to silence it with optimism. You tell yourself, "It's just a bad month," or "Things will settle after this next push." But your instinct is often the first system to detect that the business is drifting off course - even if you can't yet articulate why.

Subtle Financial Signals That Something's Off

Eventually, the emotional undercurrent is joined by measurable strain. Often, it begins with cash flow. Not because you're not making sales, but because the timing is always so tight. You're waiting on invoices.

You're dipping into personal funds or using your personal credit card(s) to cover shortfalls. Your revenue might be stable, but there's never enough liquidity to feel safe.

This is one of the most misleading stages of decline, because on paper the business might still look viable. You're making money. But you're also constantly behind. You're robbing Peter to pay Paul. Every month is a careful dance of which supplier to pay first, which expense to delay, which direct debit to bounce temporarily. The financial system that's supposed to support your business starts to choke it instead. If guilt is your driver, with staff to pay or investors to please, or friends to prove to then it will be choking you too.

At the same time, other symptoms begin to appear. Exhaustion is no longer tied to occasional sprints - it becomes permanent. Even short breaks feel indulgent, impossible, or dangerous, because you can guarantee that something will happen while you are not there, right?! The guilt of resting becomes greater than the benefit. So you stop paying any attention to your needs. When burnout is layered on top of poor cash flow, clarity disappears. You begin to make decisions reactively instead of strategically. You patch holes instead of redesigning the system.

Often, founders push harder here. More discounts, more hours, more late night reading and research, more hustling. But despite the increased effort, income plateaus - or worse, it starts to decline. You're doing more than ever and getting less in return. The pipeline dries up, or customer interest wanes. You sense that the market is shifting, but you don't have the energy to relearn how to use the new tools, pivot or adapt.

Early Warning Signs You Should Never Ignore

These red flags are often present months - sometimes even years- before a business fails:

1. Cash Flow Crunches Become the Norm

You're constantly waiting on invoices, juggling payment deadlines, or covering business expenses on personal credit cards. You may be making sales, but you never seem to have money.

2. Constant Exhaustion and Overwork

You're burning out, but there's no space to step back. Even short breaks feel impossible, in fact even a lunch break is rare. You might tell yourself it's just a "busy season," but deep down, you know it never ends.

3. Revenue Plateauing or Declining

Even if you're working harder than ever, income is stagnant- or worse, declining. You're unsure where the next customer is coming from, and your pipeline is worryingly dry.

4. Staff or Contractor Turnover

People keep leaving, unexpectedly and when it is the worst moment possible. You don't have time to recruit or maybe you don't have the budget to replace them. You end up absorbing the work, stretching thinner each month.

5. You've Stopped Investing in Growth

Applying for grant funding or looking for collaborators, and even networking events become too much of a time suck.

Training, marketing, website updates, or new offers keep getting pushed aside "until things pick up." But they never do.

6. You're Ignoring Financials

You've stopped logging into Xero or checking your bank balance. You avoid opening letters from HMRC or your accountant. Avoidance becomes a survival tactic buried deep in a drawer of your desk.

7. Customers Are Slipping Away

Repeat business drops. Leads are slower. You're getting fewer referrals. The market is changing, but your offer hasn't evolved and you just don't have time to think about it.

8.Overwhelm paralyses you

The pace of business evolution and new technology becomes an overwhelming force you just can't keep up with. You feel left behind.

When the Cracks Reach the Team

For those with a team or regular freelancers or contractors, the ripple effects become more visible. Turnover increases. People begin to disengage or your contractors just can't fit your work in. The culture you tried to build starts to erode.

Perhaps you stop replacing leavers altogether, absorbing their roles into your already full plate. Maybe you delay reviews, cancel meetings, avoid conflict.

The cracks are no longer invisible- they're structural. Still, they're easy to justify.

You tell yourself this is what happens during tight periods. That you'll fix things when cash improves. That morale dips happen in every company.

But underinvestment in your people - and in yourself - rarely ends well.

At the same time, the very parts of the business that might help reverse the slide - marketing, training, new products or services, new automated systems and processes - fall by the wayside. You put off that website refresh. You delay launching the new service. You stop investing in everyone's professional development. You don't save yourself time by automating your invoicing or learn how to use AI to build out the sales or investor decks. Growth becomes a future plan, not a current priority.

When Avoidance Becomes a Strategy

Another common signal that things are deteriorating is avoidance. You start ignoring your own numbers. You stop logging into your accounting software.

You delete unread emails from your bookkeeper. You avoid HMRC brown envelopes like they're radioactive. You delay updates to your investors or board members, or gloss over the issues hoping that things will stabilise on their own.

Avoidance isn't laziness. It's self-protection. It's your mind trying to shield you from the discomfort of facing a truth you're not ready to handle. But what gets avoided only grows.

The unspoken becomes unmanageable. The thing you couldn't look at becomes the thing you can no longer control.

And while this is happening internally, there's often a parallel shift in customer behaviour.

Repeat business begins to fade. Referrals dry up. Engagement drops. Clients start ghosting. Your offer, once relevant and in demand, no longer quite hits the mark- but you haven't evolved it because you've been too overwhelmed just keeping things going.

Operational Systems Begin to Strain

When the business begins to break under pressure, it's not just emotions or money that reflect the tension. It's the systems.

You begin to miss deadlines, or double book meetings, or delivery slows. Customers complain more. Tech breaks and doesn't get fixed. Admin piles up. Processes that were fragile to begin with start collapsing entirely. What was once manageable chaos becomes actual disorder. You're now spending more time correcting errors than creating value.

You may even find yourself taking on work that's completely outside your usual service just to keep cash coming in.

You say yes to things you don't enjoy, that don't align with your brand, and that leave you feeling further disconnected from your original purpose. But you're in survival mode. Purpose always comes second to survival.

These aren't just inconvenient. They're indicators that your business model or setup might need urgent adjustment.

Why Founders Are Often the Last to Know

What's heartbreaking - and deeply human - is that most founders don't see the whole picture until it's dangerously late. One of the most common issues among small business owners is **normalising struggle**.

In the early stages of a business, long hours, late nights, and inconsistent income are often expected. But as I've pointed out already for many, those temporary sacrifices become permanent operating conditions.

One of the cruelest parts of business decline is that when you're in the thick of it, your brain isn't working at full capacity. You're reactive, emotional, foggy. You can't zoom out or make bold decisions - because you're just trying to get through the day.

That's why these early warning signs I've flagged in this chapter matter so much. If anything in this chapter feels familiar, catch those points and look at where they are trying to take you. These warning signs and areas of uncomfortable familiarity give you a chance to shift gears before the panic sets in. Because when you're deep in the red, or three months behind on VAT, or losing your best team member to burnout - it's a lot harder to get back to clarity.

I know you might not realise you're even in trouble. You're in the middle of it. Too close to have perspective. Too emotionally attached to be neutral. Too invested in the vision to accept that it might not be working. And because you've adapted to discomfort for so long, it will likely take a major crisis - a missed payroll, a funding rejection, a key team member's resignation, or a client that inexplicitly walks away - for reality to land.

Even then, you may rationalise. "Every business has slow seasons." "Other people have been through worse."

"This is just temporary." You begin gaslighting yourself, trying to turn intuition into paranoia and struggle into hustle. You compare yourself to others and assume you're simply not trying hard enough.

But the truth is, effort isn't always the answer. Sometimes, the most courageous thing you can do is stop and look honestly at what's happening.

The Gut Instinct You Don't Trust Anymore

You genuinely will feel it before you can explain it. A subtle disconnection from your business. A sense of dread when you check your inbox. An invisible weight in your chest when you talk about the future.

This isn't just anxiety - it's your instinct trying to speak to you. Every founder who's been through this has a moment. The one where it hits them: I can't keep going like this.

For some, it's a client calling to chase work you forgot to deliver. For others, it's a rejected loan application, or the sinking feeling of not being able to pay yourself again.

The moment varies. But the emotion is the same: the realisation that the way you've been operating is no longer working.

That moment hurts. But catch it, it's also the doorway to change.

Too often, founders override this voice. They push through. They rationalise the signs away. But when your intuition tells you something's wrong, listen.

It doesn't always mean closure - it might mean something needs to shift. **I was afraid to admit it wasn't working. Not just to others - but to myself.**

This is why external perspective matters. A coach, mentor, accountant, or even a brutally honest friend, child or parent can often spot the signs you're missing.

The Power of Naming It - What Awareness Makes Possible

Sometimes, the most powerful thing you can do is admit the truth.

Saying, "I'm struggling," or "This isn't working," or even, "I don't know what to do next," takes courage. But it's the first step toward doing something different.

When you name the issue, you can work with it. You can ask for help. You can look at your options. You can take a breath.

You're no longer stuck in the swirl of shame and stories. You're in reality - and that's where all good decisions are made.

The moment you admit something is wrong is the moment you create the possibility of change. Clarity is uncomfortable - but it's genuinely freeing.

When you allow yourself to step back, to zoom out from the daily grind, you really begin to see the patterns. You can spot where the tension is building. You can face the numbers without shame. You can talk to someone who sees you clearly - a coach, an advisor, a peer who won't let you hide behind "I'm fine."

You begin to question what you've been pouring energy into that hasn't been working. You notice which part of your offer never really gained traction. You can see that the tech issues point to a bigger problem in the team and the product. You identify which marketing channels drain more than they deliver. And instead of doubling down, you let go. You clear space.

This isn't easy. But it's essential.

Collapse may begin quietly - but so does recovery. And the earlier you intervene, the softer the landing can be.

What to Do If You See the Cracks

1. **Pause and zoom out.** Step away from the daily grind. Look at the bigger picture. What's really going on? Step back and review the whole picture. Not just sales. Look at profit, workload, wellbeing, team, customers, and trends. Where is the tension building?

2. **Get honest with your numbers.** You don't need to do a full audit. Just understand what's coming in, what's going out, and what's overdue.

Assess how long you could operate at your current pace.

3. **Stop Pouring Into What Isn't Working.** That offer that never sells? The tech that still doesn't work? That marketing channel that drains your time? Let it go. Free up energy.

4. **Pick one thing to fix.** Don't try to solve everything in one weekend. Choose one area - like cash flow, or your offer, or your schedule- and focus there.

5. **Speak to Someone.** You don't have to do this alone. Speaking out loud often creates space for solutions.

6. **Start small.** The road back doesn't begin with a grand plan. It starts with one clear, grounded action.

7. **Don't Panic- Plan.** Crisis doesn't have to mean chaos. You may be able to pivot, simplify, pause, or restructure. But only if you face the reality of what's happening.

Checklist: Spotting the Cracks

- ☐ I've noticed repeated late payments or cash gaps
- ☐ I avoid checking my financials or accounts
- ☐ I'm working more but earning the same (or less)
- ☐ I feel tired, stuck, or secretly resentful of the business
- ☐ I'm doing work outside of what I want to be known for
- ☐ I have a growing sense that something needs to change

If three or more of these feel familiar, pause. Don't panic. But don't ignore it either.

Facing the Truth Isn't Giving Up

If you're here, reading this, and nodding along, I want you to know: you're not broken. Your business isn't doomed. You're just hitting the point where something needs to shift.

And the good news? That's completely normal.

This chapter isn't here to scare you. It's here to empower you. Recognising early warning signs doesn't mean giving up - Recognising that your business is struggling doesn't mean you've failed. It means you're finally giving yourself a chance to respond. It means you care enough to look. It means you're willing to lead through truth instead of denial.

Whether the next step is a pivot, a pause, a restructure, or a winding-down process, the decision will be stronger for having been made in clarity.

You can't fix what you won't face. But when you do face it- fully, honestly, and with support- something shifts. You reclaim your power. You return to the helm.

And even if the ship changes course, it's because you chose it-not because you ignored the storm.

"Every collapse starts with a crack. But every recovery starts with awareness."

Now let's look at the key problem areas and how you can tackle them if they have shown up for you.

Chapter 2

Cash Flow Chaos - When Numbers Stop Adding Up

When Sales Aren't the Problem - But the Bank Balance Is.

You can be making sales, bringing in clients, and seeing decent turnover- and still feel like you are on the brink of disaster, staring down the barrel of a bank account that's running on fumes. Sound's dramatic doesn't it but it's one of the most common (and most confusing) experiences for small business owners and if it sounds familiar, you're not alone.Cash flow issues are among the most common reasons small businesses fail, especially in the UK. And yet, they often come as a surprise. On paper, you're doing fine, everyone thinks you have a roaring success on your hands. The invoices are out. The orders are coming in. Yet somehow, your bank account tells a very different story.

That's the strange, frustrating paradox of cash flow - it's not about how much you earn. It's about when the money lands, how fast it leaves, and whether you're left with enough to keep the lights on.You might have heard that saying: "Turnover is vanity. Profit is sanity. Cash is reality." It's become cliché in some circles, but only because it's so often proven true. You can have a wildly successful month on paper and still not have the money to pay your rent. You can be "growing" and still be broke. It's not helped by a culture of blue chip corporates who seem to survive on huge debt and losses yet still manage to pay shareholders and owners dividends and fat cat salaries, It's a bizarre contradiction - until you understand how cash flow really works.

And if you don't get a handle on it, it can sink your business-fast.

Cashflow challenges can be created by many things that we will explore throughout this book.

But this chapter explores specifically why cash flow itself is the number one killer of small businesses in the UK.

I will go through how to spot the signs early, how to get a grip on your money without needing a finance degree, and what practical steps you can take to create breathing room - even in the tightest of months.

This is your guide to understanding what's really going on when the numbers don't add up, even though the business is technically "growing." We'll look at the early signs of cash flow chaos, what creates these mismatches between revenue and reality, and how to take back control - even if spreadsheets aren't your thing.Most importantly, this chapter is here to remind you that you don't need a finance degree or even someone working alongside you with a finance degree to get a handle on your money. You just need visibility, clarity, and some regular, no-nonsense practices that help you stay in control - even when the months are tight.

But you do need to stop avoiding your bank balance.

Understanding Cash Flow (And Why Profit Isn't Enough)

Let's get one thing straight right away: **Profit ≠ Cash Flow.**

Profit is what you're left with after you subtract your expenses from your revenue. But cash flow is the actual movement of money - what's coming into your bank account, what's leaving, and when those movements happen.

You can be profitable on paper and still not have any money in your bank account. Because while profit looks nice on paper, it doesn't pay your rent. It doesn't cover your staff costs. And it definitely doesn't stop the taxman from sending that dreaded brown envelope.

Profit is what's left over after you have paid out on all your expenses. Cash flow is what's actually moving - what's entering and leaving your account in real time, literally on the daily.

And you can technically "lose" money one month but still have cash reserves that keep you stable. That's why cash is king. You can't pay your staff with future profits. You pay them with the money you have right now. It's entirely possible to be technically "profitable" and still be unable to pay your bills. Because if the money hasn't hit your account yet - or if it's going out faster than it's coming in - your business is in trouble.

And here's the kicker: many business owners don't realise how tight their cash flow really is until it's too late. If your business is always teetering, if you're always waiting for that one invoice, or grant or advance payment to land so you can pay bills, it's not just stressful - it's dangerous. And it's more common than most founders want to admit.

"Turnover is vanity. Profit is sanity. Cash is reality." - Old business saying (that's 100% true)

You don't run a business on profit. You run it on **cash in the bank**.

Why Small Businesses Struggle With Cash Flow

So if cash flow is this important, why do so many businesses get it wrong?

Because it's messy. Because it's emotional. Because a lot of us were never taught about money in school or in our families. And because we're often trained via all those well meaning accelerators out there to focus on growth and investment, not stability, sales and timing. But knowing where your money is - and how long it'll last - is what keeps your doors open.

Here are the most common reasons small businesses, especially in the UK, fall into cash flow trouble:

1. Payment Terms Delay Income

If you work with other businesses, you're probably all too familiar with 30-day terms - or worse, 60 or 90 often imposed by corporates. You do the work, send the invoice, and wait. And wait. And wait some more. All the while, your bills keep coming. Even if you're invoicing clients on just 30-day terms, and they regularly pay late (as many do), despite legislation to try and prevent this, you could be waiting 60 days or more for money that was supposed to land weeks ago. If you invoice after doing the work this hurts even more, and in the meantime, you're covering expenses from your own reserves. This lag creates a painful cash flow gap - especially if you've already paid for staff, software, stock, or services to deliver the work in the first place.

2. Irregular or Seasonal Income

Freelancers, consultants, and product-based businesses often have feast-or-famine income. You have a finite amount of time, or product to sell. One month you're flush. The next, you're watching your balance dwindle. Predictable cash flow is rare - and without planning, those famine months can sink you.

3. Overheads That Outpace Revenue

Growth is exciting - but it also eats cash. Maybe you've taken on new staff, a bigger office, or more tools to manage the load. But if your income doesn't scale up just as fast (or faster), you'll feel the pinch quickly.

Rent, salaries, subscriptions, packaging, software - the list goes on. One small price increase or a new hire, and suddenly your monthly outgoings are bigger than your inflows. Growth can actually cause a cash crunch if you're not careful, especially under the pressure you might feel from investors to spend your cash to drive growth.

4. No Cash Flow Forecast

This one's big. So many small business owners have no idea what's coming in or going out until it happens. They can't use their bookkeeping software themselves, they don't know the difference between the reports, and there's no three-month cash projection. No plan for VAT or corporation tax, or employers PAYE, or pension payments that add to staff salaries. No emergency fund. You're flying blind - and that's terrifying.

If you don't have a clear view of your income and expenses over the next few months, you can't see a problem coming until it's already here. Without a forecast, you're not managing your business - you're literally guessing.

5. Paying Yourself Too Much (or Not At All)

Some months, you pay yourself generously. Others, you skip a paycheck to cover expenses. There's no consistency, no clear plan. And that instability bleeds into every other part of your decision-making. Some founders pay themselves too generously from the start, to try and match their old corporate salary, or cut their salary too much on an investor's demands, pay themselves last and go months without a paycheck. Neither is sustainable.

You need consistency and planning to keep your business - and yourself - financially stable.

6. Paying for things you really don't need

Oh that influx of cash...when it does come, it can feel so good when you have literally been living like a student for a long time...but you aren't a student anymore, this isn't a splurge and starve scenario guys, it is real grown up life and you do not need the pool table, the fancy laptops or the pricey coffee machine to run the business, but you do need cash. Your investors will pressure you to spend it but you need to be careful and only spend it on the things that really matter.

The Warning Signs of Cash Flow Chaos

Even before you see red in your bank account, the signs are there:

- You're constantly transferring money between accounts
- You're using credit cards or loans from anyone you can get to help, to cover operating expenses
- You hold off on paying invoices and suppliers until the very last minute
- You dread payday or VAT deadlines
- You avoid looking at your banking app or checking it at all
- You genuinely have no idea how much money is coming in next month

Sound familiar?

Here's how one e-commerce founder put it:

"We were selling out some of our products every month. But because I'd over-committed to new stock, I couldn't stock up on what was selling out"

This is how it happens. Slowly. Quietly. And then- suddenly. You think everything's fine - until it isn't.

The Reality Behind the Numbers - A Simple Example

Let's say you run a creative agency.

You invoice a client £5,000 on 1st June, with 30-day payment terms. But the client pays late and the money doesn't land until mid-July.

Meanwhile, in June:

- You pay £1,000 to a subcontractor
- £1,500 in rent
- £500 in software and subscriptions
- £800 to yourself

That's £3,800 out - before the £5,000 even hits your account. On paper, June looks profitable. But in real life, you're in the red and very cash negative until that invoice is paid, and if they are late you are scrabbling. You're relying on a credit card, overdraft, or sheer hope to stay upright.

This is the trap. Profit tells one story. Cash flow tells the truth.

Getting a Grip: Understanding Your Cash Flow

The good news? You can fix this. You don't need any finance qualifications or training. You just need a few simple tools - and a willingness to look. To regain control, you need to start tracking all cash in and out literally daily if you have to - this is not just about income and expenses, it is every tiny thing and easily found on your bank statement from last month, and in simple reports in your bookkeeping software or order/supplier book.

1. Use a Cash Flow Forecast

This can be as simple as a spreadsheet or built into software like Xero, QuickBooks, or Float. The goal is to see what's coming up before it hits you in the face. I have a template you can access from the link at the back of the book.

You need to track:

- Expected income (by date it will likely arrive, not just amount)
- Committed outgoings (fixed costs, wages, VAT, etc by when they need to be paid.)
- Variable costs (stock, freelancers, deliveries, etc by when they will need to be paid.)
- Tax and VAT deadlines
- Bank balance at the start of each month

Update this weekly. Look at the next 3–6 months. It's like checking the weather before you plan a picnic - just with fewer ants.

2. Know Your Break-Even Point

How much do you need to earn **each month** just to cover basic operations (not grow or save- just survive)? That's your survival baseline. If you don't know it you're guessing.

3. Understand Your Cash Conversion Cycle

How long does it take from selling something to having the money in your account? Or in other words, how long does it take between spending money to get the client/or the sale and getting it back? Shorten this cycle wherever you can. The shorter this cycle, the healthier your cash flow.

Look for ways to reduce the gap - like faster invoicing, up-front deposits, or retainer agreements. Faster cash flow = more flexibility. Speed this up wherever possible.

Fixing the Leaks: Short-Term Cash Strategies

If you're already feeling the squeeze, here are some immediate tactics to stabilise and literally buy yourself some breathing room:

1. Speed up payments

- If you are selling a product make the first 10/40/100 cheaper than the next batch
- Incentivise early payment for services with small discounts (e.g. 5% discount for paying within 7 days)
- Make it normal to get 50% of fees up front and give a lower price for full payment up front or a higher price if the customer wants you to provide something faster.
- Add late payment fees (and actually enforce them)
- Send reminders before invoices are due - not just after they're late
- Chase overdue invoices assertively don't wait three weeks to chase

2. Reduce Your Business Outgoings

- Pause non-essential tools or subscriptions
- Move from annual to monthly billing for everything you can
- Renegotiate supplier contracts or switch providers
- Sublet part of your office or a parking space

3. Improve Pricing & Payment Terms

- As suggested above, ask for partial payment up front like a 50% deposit
- Shorten payment terms to 14 days or 'by return' where possible
- Reassess your pricing structure and renegotiate prices if your margin is too thin (you may be undercharging)
- Bundle services for faster, lower-lift offers that get paid quickly.

4. Free Up Stock or Services

- Run a quick-fire sale on old inventory
- Offer 'quick win' services or mini packages
- Sell unused equipment or assets

Long-Term Resilience: Building a Cash Buffer

The real win isn't just fixing cash flow once with a short term fix - it's building systems that protect you in the future and give you long term resilience to stop the problem happening again.

1. Create a "No Matter What" Fund

Even a £1,000 buffer can change how you make decisions. Aim for 1–3 months of core expenses over time. Keep it in a separate account- out of sight, out of mind. It's your oxygen mask in a crisis.

2. Build Recurring Revenue Streams

Can you add a retainer model? A subscription? A service plan? Predictable monthly income is peace of mind, it helps smooth out your cash flow and reduces stress.

Even a barber in my local town has set up a subscription model £100 p/month for up to four haircuts a month, with priority booking and it is working a treat for him.

3. Try Profit First Principles

By prioritizing profit, you're forcing yourself to manage the business on what's left, which naturally leads to leaner operations and smarter spending. Regularly transferring money into a separate Profit Account builds a financial buffer, ensuring that your business isn't just surviving but thriving.This model (from Mike Michalowicz's book) involves dividing every bit of income into separate buckets:

- Profit
- Owner's Pay
- Taxes
- Operating Expenses

So essentially you literally divide every bit of your revenue/income to split between these categories. Even allocating 1% to that profit box can shift your financial habits.

Avoiding Common Cash Flow Mistakes (that are totally avoidable)

STOP....

- Assuming revenue growth = cash (growth often eats cash)
- Relying on overdrafts, loans or credit without a plan
- Ignoring tax liabilities until the last minute
- Paying yourself only from leftovers (unsustainable and often nothing)

- Outsourcing finances entirely to a bookkeeper without understanding basics

You don't need to be an accountant. But you **do need visibility**. Founders who understand cash flow sleep better, lead better and make clearer decisions.

If You're Already in the Red

First of all- breathe (and stop panicking). This happens. And it doesn't make you a failure.

1. Don't hide. Avoidance makes it worse. Open the bank app. Look at the numbers. Make a list.

2. Prioritise payments. Figure out what absolutely needs to be paid now - HMRC, staff, key suppliers? Be honest and upfront with those you owe, try and agree to a payment plan of some sort that is fair to everyone (including you).

3. Talk to someone. Speak to someone who you can ask for clarity and not judgement. Your accountant, your coach, even your most trusted business friend. Even Citizen's Advice will give you advice if you are a small business or business owner.

4. Explore Support

- **Business overdrafts** (as a bridge, so short-term only)
- **Startup loans** (gov-backed based on a Director's credit position)
- **Community grants or local enterprise support** (free advice is available from every UK council and their business support team)
- **Payment plans with HMRC** for VAT or Corporation Tax arrears

"The moment I sat down and built a forecast - even though the picture was bleak- I felt relief. I had a map. I could make choices again."

You don't need to fix it overnight but you do need to act quickly. And you have options but you do also need a plan.

A Final Word: This Is More Common Than You Think

Cash flow chaos doesn't mean you're bad at business. It means you're doing too much, too fast, with too little room to breathe. That's the point of this chapter - not to scare you, but to give you your map.

Checklist: Managing Cash Flow

- ☐ I have a 3–6 month cash forecast
- ☐ I check my cash position weekly
- ☐ I understand my break-even point
- ☐ I invoice promptly and follow up regularly
- ☐ I have a plan for slow months
- ☐ I know exactly what I need to earn this month

If you can't tick most of these - don't panic. Pick one. Start there. Progress doesn't require perfection. It just needs honesty.

Because you don't need perfect numbers. You need real ones. That's where clarity begins.

Interlude - What They Wish You Knew... Cashflow Pressure: The Silent Killer of Good Businesses

Advice from the Morpheus of the accounting world - Laurence Fishman - Nyman Libson Paul LLP Chartered Accountants.

"I THINK we're ok..."

If those words have ever crossed your lips as a founder, you already know you're absolutely not. When it comes to cashflow, hope is not a strategy.

The number at the top of your online banking screen might look fine, but it doesn't tell you about the VAT bill landing next week, the three invoices still unpaid, or payroll waiting around the corner.

Cash doesn't run out suddenly. It leaks. Slowly at first, then all at once. The problem isn't just the absence of money — it's the absence of foresight and timely action.

The 12-Week Forecast

The most powerful discipline I've seen in my clients is a 12-week rolling cashflow forecast. Every in, every out, every invoice, every payroll run. Line by line. Updated weekly.

This isn't some boring finance chore — it's oxygen. Like a baby, your cash flow needs routine, care and constant attention. At first, you'll resist it. But the clarity that comes is a game-changer. Suddenly you can see which customers are always late, which expenses drain value, and exactly how much time you have to plug the gaps.

Visibility turns blind panic into focus. It gives you breathing space.

The Real Enemy

Founders often tell me: "we just need more sales." In reality, sales volume is rarely the true cause of a cash squeeze.

The real enemy is inertia:

- Too slow chasing late payers.
- Too slow cutting what's not working.
- Too slow rethinking pricing.
- Too slow stopping panic payments.

A week's delay can be more lethal than a bad quarter.

The Psychology of Pressure

The uncertainty is crippling. I've seen brilliant founders lie awake at 3 a.m. wondering if payroll will clear. And pride makes it worse - nobody wants to admit the "everything's great" façade is cracking.

But here's the truth: every founder you admire has felt it too. Especially the ones who look invincible. And when you use that pressure well, it sharpens decision-making like nothing else.

Margins Matter More Than Sales

Margins are not just another number. They're the buffer between floating and drowning.

A £2m business at 5% margin has £100,000 to play with. A £1m business at 30% margin has £300,000. I know which I'd rather be running.

Top-line growth feeds ego. Strong margins feed survival.

The Discipline That Wins

Cashflow discipline isn't glamorous, but it's what keeps businesses alive. The founders who win are not always the smartest - but they are the fastest to act:

- They check numbers weekly.
- They chase invoices without shame.
- They trim fat before it turns flabby.
- They raise prices when costs demand it, and own the increase.

Do this consistently and the monster under your bed just becomes part of the job. Cashflow management isn't a shackle; it's a guardrail keeping you on track when things get bumpy.

Final Wish

So here's my wish for you:

May your invoices land quickly, your margins stay healthy, and your bank balance brings more smiles than headaches.

And if you're still not sure you've got this - I know a really great accountant who can help.

Chapter 3

Customer Drought - The Disappearing Demand

When the Crowd Goes Quiet

There's a particular kind of silence that sends a chill through the spine of even the most seasoned business owner. It's not dramatic. There's no big alarm bell, no flashing red light. Just a subtle quietness. The inbox that used to ping with enquiries now sits still. The usual bump in website traffic seems to have flattened out. Sales, once a familiar and comforting rhythm, are now intermittent - sometimes entirely absent. You start checking your notifications more often, hoping for a ping that never comes...

At first, you reason it away. Maybe it's the school holidays. Maybe the algorithm's being weird again. Maybe it's just a quiet week. It happens, right? But then a week turns into two. A month passes. And the energy that used to buzz around your business starts to feel like it's evaporating. You keep refreshing your analytics, rereading customer emails, scrolling back through old social media posts that used to spark excitement, wondering if you should be contributing to the AI slop machine with automatic posts - you are literally hunting for clues as to why your marketing isn't working and your customers have stopped buying.

What's frightening is how common this is. When I first started digging into why small businesses fail, the statistic that stopped me in my tracks was this: 64% of businesses don't have effective marketing. Not poor products. Not terrible service. Just a lack of strategy around visibility, messaging, and connection. That's the root cause of failure for most. The customers don't always disappear because they no longer care - they disappear because the business stopped reaching them in a way that cut through.

And let's face it with AI in the mix that is even harder, especially when you don't know how to use it or how to know if this is why you aren't getting the business you used to get.

Here's the hard part: most founders don't notice that their customers just aren't engaging, and new leads aren't coming by, people don't want their product anymore and that their old marketing approach isn't working until the silence has settled in.

Welcome to customer drought - a slow, creeping erosion of interest and demand that can destabilise a small business before the founder even realises what's happening.

And the worst part? You're not quite sure what caused it - or how to fix it.

In this chapter, we'll explore how and why customer interest disappears, how to tell whether it's temporary or systemic, and what you can do to win back attention, loyalty, and sustainable demand before your business dries up entirely.

Understanding the Drought: what it really means.

A customer drought doesn't always mean something's gone terribly wrong. Often, it's a sign that the ground beneath your business has shifted - often very quietly, subtly, and without a memo. The habits and expectations of your audience might have changed. Economic pressures may have pulled the rug out from under what used to be a reliable flow of spending. Your once-unique offer might now be surrounded by a sea of similar options. Competitors have adopted a new approach. And suddenly, the tried-and-tested no longer feels tried - or tested.

The things you have always done to reach your customers just don't work anymore.

When the world changes, businesses need to change with it. But that's easier said than done, especially when you're juggling a thousand plates already. Most small businesses don't have the luxury of a research and development team or a marketing department monitoring customer trends. It could even be just you, maybe a virtual assistant or a freelancer or two, and a lot of instinct.

But instinct can be dulled when you're in survival mode. When you're busy working **in** the business, you don't always have time to work **on** it. So when the drop in engagement begins - fewer likes, fewer opens, fewer sales - you might not notice right away. And by the time you do, it can feel like the well has already dried up.

Still, drought doesn't mean death. It means pause. It means shift. It means adapt. Sometimes, you're not failing. You're just out of step. And this chapter is here to help you get back in rhythm.

A customer drought doesn't always mean you've failed. Often, and especially likely in the climate today, it means the **landscape has shifted**:

- Customer behaviours evolve
- Economic conditions tighten spending
- Competitors enter the market
- Attention spans shrink
- Your offer stops meeting the moment
- Your product isn't meeting the needs of the market
- Your product isn't ready yet

The signs are subtle at first: lower email open rates, slower conversion, reduced engagement on social, longer sales cycles. But over time, they snowball into serious revenue problems.

"We were doing all the same things - same digital ads, same emails, same content - but nothing was landing. It felt like the whole market had gone silent."
- Independent retail founder, Manchester

How to Spot a Drought Before It Hits Hard

Let's be honest - many of us don't realise we're in a drought until we're deep in the desert, rationing whatever drops are left in the flask. The sooner you spot the signs, the easier it is to turn things around. But spotting those signs requires one thing above all else: attention.

Are you noticing a dip in repeat purchases? Are customers ghosting after one interaction? Have you quietly stopped getting referrals, testimonials, or enthusiastic emails from happy buyers? Maybe your sales have slowed, but you haven't had the headspace to dig into 'why'.

Ignoring these clues is understandable- especially if you're tired, overwhelmed, or in deep "hustle" mode. But turning a drought around starts with seeing it clearly. Looking your numbers in the eye. Listening to your gut. And, more importantly, reaching out to your customers to understand their experience, instead of guessing from behind the safety of a screen.

The good news is you can use technology to really understand what the shift is for your products and your market very quickly. You can do this today. Let's look at the likely causes of a shift in customer engagement and demand first.

Common Causes of Demand Disappearance

1. Market Saturation

What was once unique is now everywhere. New competitors emerge. The novelty wears off what you are selling is a 'same as' not a new thing anymore.

2. Misaligned Messaging

You're saying the same things - but your audience's priorities have changed as they have changed. Your offer just doesn't resonate the way it used to.

3. Pricing vs. Perceived Value

Customers no longer see your product or service as "worth it." Not always because of quality - but because their budget or expectations have shifted.

4. Neglected Audience

Maybe you've been so focused on operations that you've stopped engaging your audience. They've drifted to someone more visible, consistent, or connected.

5. Economic Conditions

Inflation, cost of living, interest rates - all affect consumer behaviour. People think harder before buying, delay purchases, or trade down.

Diagnosing the Root Cause: Don't Just Guess - Investigate

So, you've spotted the signs. You've accepted the silence isn't just a phase. Now what?

The worst thing you can do at this point is to throw spaghetti at the wall - posting more, discounting everything, changing your whole offer overnight - without knowing what's actually going wrong. Because what if it's not your offer? What if the issue is that people don't know you exist? Or that your message is missing the mark?

Diagnosing a customer drought requires curiosity and a bit of humility. It's time to get out of your own head - and into the heads of your customers. And that means you have to actually reach out to people. Not via email or text.

Start by talking to people - in real life. Not just through surveys or comment boxes. Actual conversations. Whether it's hopping on a 10-minute call with a past client or sending a personal message asking for verbal feedback, there's gold in hearing how people think, feel, and decide.

Ask them questions like:
- What made you stop engaging?
- What's changed in your world recently?
- What would make this product or service feel more relevant right now?

You'll likely hear patterns - things that hadn't occurred to you, or shifts you weren't aware of.
This information is priceless, especially when your instinct might have told you to fix something that wasn't broken.

Next, audit your funnel - in case you don't know, this is your customer journey from first contact to final sale. If you do know, then look in detail at the marketing and sales touchpoints and stages your customers go through on their journey to buy from you.

Even if it is a shop window, something draws people into your shop. If it is a high tech product or service - where are you finding people who need you, what do they respond to that you expect to pull them to your website to buy your product, what happens at every stage of their journey to find you - do you really know where people are slipping away?

Check the analytics aligned to your website. Are people landing on your website but not buying? Which pages seem to get the most attention, which don't. Are they adding things to their cart and ghosting? Why might that be, is it hard to complete a purchase?

Look at your incoming calls and your live customers. Are you having calls that don't convert? Are people buying once but never returning?

Each leak in the funnel needs its own attention. Don't waste energy fixing what isn't broken. Zero in on the stage where the drop-off is happening. A poor website, understanding your customers needs, or a leaky funnel that drives customers to your business, are not unsolvable problems when you can ask a free AI chat tool for tips and advice to help you improve your approach.

But let's take each piece at a time, because whether you use technology to help the principles still apply.

Taking an Honest Look at Messaging

First think about who you are talking to - who is your ideal customer, the typical one, who buys most of your products or services and who you think about when you are thankful you have a few regular customers you can (or could) count on. What are you saying to them in the way you present your business, what is their life like today and how might things have changed for them in recent times?

Messaging is one of the most overlooked areas in a business. It's not just what you say - it's how you say it, when you say it, and whether it still resonates. What connected with people a year ago might not land today. Language needs to evolve as your audience evolves.

If your messaging is too focused on features and what you are selling, instead of benefits that the person you are selling to will experience from engaging with you, or if the story you tell is about your business rather than about your customer, it may fall flat. If it's vague, outdated, or overly polished, people might scroll past.

In a world full of noise, being real with clarity and honesty cuts through.

Read your website aloud. Check your bios on social media. Listen to your last few sales calls or pitches. Does your message match where your customer is now? Are you sure? Or is it speaking to a version of them that no longer exists?

Competitor Activity: Not to Copy- But to Learn

Spying on your competition isn't about copying their content or mimicking their branding. It's about understanding the game you're playing.

What are others in your space doing differently? Are they addressing a shift in customer need that you've missed? Are they offering better packaging, clearer pricing, more empathy in their marketing?

You're not here to play catch-up. But awareness helps you pivot smartly. Sometimes, the answer isn't to shout louder - it's to say something different.

Just running these questions through an AI chatbot referencing your own website, and naming those competitors you do know about and bingo...insights!

Diagnostic checklist

Before you try to fix anything, you need clarity on what's *actually* happening.

1. Talk to Your Customers

Not just surveys - real conversations. What's changed for them? What are they looking for now? Why did they stop buying or stop showing interest in your new product/tech?

2. Review Your Funnel

Where are people dropping off?

- Website traffic but no enquiries?
- Enquiries but no sales?
- Sales but no repeat purchases?

The stage with the biggest leak is where to focus.

3. Audit Your Messaging

Is your website, copy, and content still speaking to current needs - or stuck in the past?

4. Review Competitor Activity

What are they offering? How are they framing value? Are they gaining ground with your audience?

Reigniting Demand: The Human Way

Once you know what's not working, you can begin to fix it. But let's be clear - this isn't about manipulating people into buying. It's about reconnecting with them in a genuine, thoughtful way. This is critical in the age of AI generated messaging and content that we have already mentioned. You must keep your authentic voice and focus on your customers' real needs.

Start by simply showing up again. That might mean getting back on social media with honest, valuable content that really shows you know what people genuinely need of you and your products or services. This is not just "buy now" posts. Or send a personal email to your list sharing what's been going on behind the scenes.

Transparency builds trust. Trust builds sales. If your product or service needs a refresh, think about what would make it more appealing right now. Could it be repositioned to meet a more urgent need? Could you simplify the offer, split it into smaller chunks, or bundle it for more value? People buy what they understand - and what feels helpful.

You can also re-engage past customers. A check-in message, a loyalty offer, or even a genuine "we've missed you" note can reignite relationships. The people who already know and like you are the warmest audience you have. Don't overlook them in the chase for new leads.

And if you're going to use scarcity tactics - like limited spots or time-bound bonuses - make sure they're real. Fake urgency turns people off. But honest scarcity? That can be motivating.

Short-Term Strategies to Reignite Demand

1. Reconnect With Your Audience

Start showing up again. Share real, useful content. Be visible. Be helpful. Be human. Visibility precedes trust- and trust precedes sales.

2. Refresh Your Offer

Can you tweak your existing service to meet a more urgent or specific need? Can you split it into smaller parts, or bundle it for greater perceived value?

3. Use Scarcity Strategically

Limited-time offers, time-bound bonuses, or limited availability can drive action- if used ethically and sparingly.

4. Re-Engage Past Customers

Reach out to those who bought before. Offer something new. Ask for feedback. Invite them back in.

Future-Proofing: Build Demand That Doesn't Dry Up

I'm not a weather person but surely the best time to prepare for a drought is before the sky turns blue? To future-proof your business, you need diversity - not just in your offers, but in how you reach people before your main source of water dries up.

So the message is please don't build your whole strategy around one platform or one lead source. Instagram is great - until your account gets hacked or engagement drops. Word-of-mouth is golden - but not if your network dries up.

Spread your reach:

- SEO can be done using AI to help you identify key words to use on your website, or will even give you a full report in seconds to help you improve your SEO ranking and increase the chances of customers finding you,
- Email is always a strong method to engage people, but be real and to the point,
- Partnerships where you both genuinely can get something out of sharing a message, event or set of products can be worth putting effort into,
- Live events will get you in front of people fast,
- Podcast guesting to talk about your customers problems and authentically convey your understanding of these,
- Press or socials to do the same

You don't need to do all of them, pick two to give you a strong start.

Next, build a brand that people remember. That doesn't mean a slick logo. It means standing for something. Why do you do what you do? What are you willing to say that others won't? What makes your business meaningful, not just marketable?

Be human and real, engage deeply with your people. Prioritise relationships over reach. Ten thousand followers don't mean much if none of them care. But a few hundred truly connected customers? That's where the magic happens.

And don't forget the experience. The best marketing is a product or service that delights. When people feel seen, cared for, and surprised in a good way - they talk. And that kind of word-of-mouth beats any sales funnel.

Long-Term Prevention Tips: Building Demand Resilience

1. Diversify Your Channels

Relying on Instagram or one referral partner? Risky. Spread your lead sources: SEO, PR, partnerships, networking, email. Pick two - do them well then add more.

2. Build a Stronger Brand Story

People buy from businesses they understand and remember. Strengthen your positioning. What do you stand for?

What makes you different? Be public about this on social media; FaceBook, TikTok, Instagram, LinkedIn.

3. Deepen Relationships, Not Just Reach

Focus on connection over clicks. A smaller, engaged list is worth more than 10k silent followers.

4. Improve Customer Experience

Sometimes, the best marketing is delighting the people you've already sold to. Referrals, testimonials, and repeat business grow from satisfaction.

Knowing When It's Time to Pivot - or Walk Away

Not every drought is survivable in its current form. Sometimes, the market really has moved on. Sometimes, the thing you're selling no longer has the relevance it once did. That doesn't mean you've failed. It means you're evolving. Sometimes, demand disappears because the market has moved on.

- The product is outdated
- The audience has matured
- The economy no longer supports the offer

This doesn't make you a failure.

It makes you a founder at a crossroads. You can:

- Evolve your offer
- Shift your audience
- Start something new

The bravest thing a founder can do isn't pushing through a failing model. It's stepping back and asking: does this still make sense? Does this offer still matter? Is it time to shift my audience - or start something new?

I've worked with founders who held onto an old offer for years out of loyalty to the few customers that still bought it. The moment they let it go, a door opened. A new idea came in. A rebrand sparked fresh excitement. Revenue returned.

Letting go can be painful. But holding on too long can be worse.

Final Thoughts: This Isn't the End- It's a Turning Point

If you're in a customer drought right now, please know this: it's not a reflection of your worth. It's not a verdict on your product or your passion. It's feedback. It's data. It's a prompt to pause and recalibrate.

Every business goes through dry spells. The ones that recover - and thrive - are the ones that listen, learn, and adjust with honesty and courage.

Reconnect with your people. Realign your message. Rebuild your offer if you need to. And most importantly, believe that a quiet season doesn't mean your best work is behind you.

Sometimes, it's just the beginning of something stronger.

Checklist: Is Your Business in Customer Drought?

- ☐ Website traffic or leads have declined over 3+ months
- ☐ Social or email engagement has dropped significantly
- ☐ You're struggling to convert leads into sales
- ☐ Previous customers aren't returning
- ☐ You're seeing more "I'll think about it" or "too expensive" responses

If this sounds familiar - pause. Investigate. Reconnect. And most importantly, don't internalise silence as shame. It's data.

"Your customers haven't vanished. They've just changed. Meet them where they are now - not where they were when you started."

Interlude - What They Wish You Knew...When Your "Almost Ready" Never Arrives

This one is from me - because the one thing I was always really good at was getting my businesses to market - but despite my ability in the world of Go To Market delivery there is another warning I need to share as there is another side to the customer drought.

It's not having any water to give them.

I spent years chasing the promise of Bubbl, the immersive tech startup I co-founded. On paper, it looked unstoppable: InnovateUK grants, shiny awards, even a waiting list of agencies and brands excited to use our platform. The concept was bold - location-triggered content that could slot into any app. The future of marketing, right? Except the future never turned up.

We lived in a permanent state of "almost ready." Every time I pressed for timelines, the tech team assured me we were close. As a non-technical founder, I wanted to believe them. I didn't know enough to challenge whether "nearly" meant days, months, or years. In hindsight, it meant "not at all."

Our big break came - or should have - at the UK's biggest marketing industry event. We had the stage, the audience, the anticipation. I didn't know what we didn't have was a working product. My tech lead hadn't tested live at scale. We were forced to sit scrabbling behind the scenes manually trying to patch it together in real time. It didn't work. The demo failed. The hype collapsed. From that moment on, the venture was downhill.

This GTM lesson was brutal but simple: don't confuse the trappings of success with readiness to deliver. Awards, grants, and waiting lists don't matter if your product breaks the moment it touches reality. Test live, test ugly, test before you're comfortable. If I could go back, I'd run small pilots with real users months before the big stage. I'd risk embarrassment early to avoid humiliation later.

The red flag to watch for is the phrase "nearly ready."

If you hear it on repeat, stop.

Either you've got a capability gap you can't see, or you're being shielded from hard truths. Nearly ready is just another way of saying not ready. And in GTM, not ready means not real.

If you're building, don't wait for the perfect moment to launch. Launch before you're ready, because at least then you'll know what you've got. Bubbl taught me that the riskiest GTM strategy isn't moving too fast - it's standing still, polishing a product that never makes it out the door.

Chapter 4

Team Tangles - Team Trouble & Leadership Breakdown

When the Team Stops Working - Even If the People Don't Leave

Let's talk about culture - and I'm not talking about the beanbags and casual Fridays kind, but the real, gritty kind that determines how people behave when things get hard. It's easy to overlook, especially in small businesses, but when culture starts to crumble, the consequences are anything but small.

When your team stops functioning well, it doesn't always show up as people quitting or staging dramatic walkouts. Sometimes, the bodies stay - but the energy, motivation, and trust quietly slip out the back door. People go through the motions. Meetings get tense. Decisions take longer. And you, the founder, start wondering if it's them... or if it's you.

Here's the truth: culture is your business's operating system. It's not a motivational poster or a slide in your onboarding deck. It's how people actually behave when they're under pressure, when something goes wrong, when a deadline is looming and the customer's angry and the Wi-Fi's on the blink. It shows up in who speaks up, who stays silent, who gets credit, who takes blame, and how problems are handled. Or ignored.

And it's rarely one big thing that derails a team. It's a slow build-up. A missed thank you here. A brewing resentment there. An email that should have been a conversation. Someone scared of saying they don't know. A bit of avoidance, a pinch of micromanagement, and voilà - you've got yourself a toxic work stew.

I learned this the hard way. I prided myself on being honest, transparent, and committed to building a place people actually wanted to work. Truth and Trust was my mantle and I wore it in everything I did and said - or so I thought. But culture isn't just about your best intentions. It's about what actually happens, day in, day out.

In small businesses, this matters even more. There's no HR department buffering tension. No massive team to absorb a bad attitude. If you're a five-person crew, and one person is disengaged, that's 20% of your business quietly detaching. That's a big deal.

Let's dig into how culture goes sideways - even when you think you're doing all the right things.

Culture: Your Business's Human Operating System

This was such a hard one for me. I had such a strong commitment to those words truth and trust. I also became very good at blurring the lines between work colleagues and friendship. So I thought I had this one nailed. But culture isn't what you say your values are - it's how people behave when no one's watching.

It shows up in:

- How decisions are made
- How mistakes are handled
- How people communicate under stress
- How conflict is addressed (or avoided)
- How feedback is given (or withheld)

I don't like the word toxic, because a toxic culture doesn't mean the team is bad. It means the **norms, systems, and unspoken rules** are working against trust, safety, and performance.

And your whole team will have their own insecurities and personality traits that will play into the way things evolve. That is the bit you definitely can't control.

"Culture is not the words on the wall - it's what people do every day."

How Toxic Cultures Form in Small Businesses

In huge companies, toxic cultures can be baked in. Years of bad habits, unchecked egos, and broken systems passed around like office furniture. But in small businesses, it's rarely deliberate. It sneaks in while you're busy just trying to keep the lights on.

Sometimes, it starts with overwhelm. As a founder, you're doing everything - sales, support, invoicing, social media, probably mopping the floor too. Delegation becomes a game of hot potato. You hand off tasks without much clarity, cross your fingers, and hope for the best. The team, sensing the chaos, starts to mirror it.

Other times, it's the classic "too many hats, not enough heads" problem. Roles blur. Responsibilities get muddled. People try to help and cover for each other - until they don't. Or they sense the tension and start stepping on toes, trying to be the indispensable one that doesn't get fired. Deadlines slip. Frustration simmers. And before you know it, someone's eyeing the exit or just... emotionally checks out.

Then there's the bit nobody likes to talk about: the hard conversations that don't happen. Someone's underperforming. Someone else is clearly miserable. But you keep putting it off because things are already tense, and you don't want to make it worse or make them leave because you need them and don't have time to find a new hire. But what you avoid, festers.

What you tolerate, grows. And suddenly, your well-meaning team is walking on eggshells.

And let's not forget recognition - or the lack of it. When people go the extra mile and no one notices, they stop running when you are trying to pick up pace and stepping on toes. You don't need to throw a parade every time someone hits a deadline. But a simple "great work" can go a long way. When praise is rare, people start to feel invisible. And invisible people don't bring their best.

Inconsistent leadership adds another layer of confusion. If priorities change week to week, your team stops trying to keep up. They stop trusting the plan. Or worse - they stop caring.

If any of the following ring true then you need to take action

In large corporations, toxic culture is often institutional - decades of dysfunction. But in small businesses, it's usually more accidental. It creeps in through:

1. Founder Overwhelm

You're stretched too thin to manage properly. You delegate chaotically, skip feedback, and hope for the best. The team senses your stress and mirrors it.

2. Unclear Roles and Expectations

People wear too many hats. No one knows who's responsible for what, there are no clear job descriptions. Deadlines slip. Resentment grows.

3. Avoidance of Difficult Conversations

You let underperformance slide to keep the peace. You delay addressing tensions. Eventually, small problems become big fractures.

4. Toxic Loyalty

You keep people on, who you don't need or who can't do their jobs, because you don't want to hurt their feelings, or know they just lost a parent, or had a baby etc.....

5. Lack of Recognition

Good work goes unnoticed. Praise is rare because you are so busy you forget to mention that you saw what they did. People feel like cogs, not contributors.

6. Inconsistent Leadership

You change priorities weekly. Team members feel whiplash, it feels like you are panicking and they stop trusting the vision.

The Hidden Costs of a Dysfunctional Team

Poor culture doesn't just hurt feelings - it hurts your business. Productivity dips, because people aren't motivated. Mistakes go unspotted, because communication has broken down. Customers pick up on the tension, even if it's subtle. The energy shifts.

And here's the kicker: your best people are often the first to leave. They've got options. They don't want to spend their days battling passive-aggressive Slack messages or wondering whether today's plan will survive until Friday.

This is especially hard when in your lonely life as an entrepreneur these people became your friends, you thought, making the pain extra sharp when they up and leave for pastures new.

But friends are rarely those you have a transactional relationship with - if you are paying them then they have to be there, until they choose not to.

Meanwhile, you're left juggling more and more, jumping in to patch holes, solve disputes, and fix things that shouldn't have broken in the first place. It's exhausting. It's demoralising. And it's not scalable.

I once let someone go who'd been quietly undermining the rest of the team. I'd listened to all their excuses, given them a chance to fix their sloppiness, worried we couldn't manage without them or their tech knowledge. I knew they were in a lot of debt and had issues at home - I'd been dreading the conversation for weeks. But the moment it happened, I noticed something unexpected - the whole team relaxed. You could almost hear the collective exhale. That's when it hit me: the tension I'd been tolerating wasn't just mine to carry. It had become everyone's burden.

The exiting member of the team was relieved too. They were very uncomfortable under the spotlight and with so much riding on things they knew they couldn't deliver. And losing their job forced them to deal with the stuff at home.

And then there is the 'best friend' co-founder, business partner or senior team member who jumped in for the ride and the salary, or the promise or a dream, and then decided that it wasn't worth it. What was a transaction to them became a crutch for me and an illusion of friendship.
When they suddenly left, it left me holding a leaky bucket without enough hands to stop the leaks in my business and personally.

The reality is a poor team dynamic doesn't just affect morale - it hits your bottom line.

- **Productivity drops** because people are disengaged
- **Errors increase** because communication breaks down
- **Customers notice** the tension and lack of care
- **Retention suffers**, and the best people leave first
- **You become a bottleneck**, stepping in to fix problems constantly

It's not just stressful - it's unsustainable.

Warning Signs Your Culture Is Turning Toxic

- ☐ People work in silos or avoid collaboration
- ☐ Passive-aggressive communication or gossip
- ☐ Rising sick days, lateness, or disengagement
- ☐ Feedback is rare or always negative
- ☐ People start murmuring about being undermined or micromanaged
- ☐ You dread team meetings - or avoid them, or you notice others doing so
- ☐ You spend more time mediating than managing

If three or more feel familiar, it's time to investigate. These patterns don't fix themselves.

How Leadership Breakdown Fuels Culture Decay

Here's a tough pill to swallow: as the founder, you're setting the tone - whether you mean to or not. That doesn't mean you have to be perfect. But your mood, your decisions, your consistency (or lack of it) all shape how safe people feel, how much they trust you, and whether they feel like showing up fully.

Micromanaging sends the message that no one's trusted. Neglect tells people they're not valued. If you swing between optimism and panic, people learn to brace for impact. And if you overpromise and underdeliver - especially repeatedly, even on things like investment which is really tough to get over the line - people just stop believing what you say.

I'm not saying this to guilt-trip anyone. But if we don't look at where our own behaviour might be part of the problem, we'll never be able to change the outcome.

That doesn't mean you have to be perfect. But if you're overwhelmed, emotionally reactive, or inconsistent, the team doesn't know what to expect.

Leadership issues that commonly damage culture:

- **Micromanagement:** No one feels trusted
- **Neglect:** No one feels seen
- **Inconsistency:** No one feels safe
- **Overpromising:** No one feels respected
- **Oversharing:** People get scared

When leadership crumbles, so does culture.

The Role of the Founder in Culture Recovery

Now comes the hard part. If any of this feels uncomfortably familiar - if you've let things slide, avoided issues, fallen out with key members of the team or simply been too burnt out to notice - you're not alone. But you are the one who has to fix it.

Owning the culture you've created doesn't mean you failed. It means you're aware. And that awareness is what gives you the power to change it.

Start by asking yourself a few hard questions: Where have I dropped the ball? What behaviours have I quietly allowed to continue,
even when I knew better? What feedback have I ignored - or been too scared to seek?

The answers might sting. That's okay. This isn't about beating yourself up. It's about stepping back into leadership, with clarity and compassion.

That starts with honesty.

Ask yourself:

- Where have I dropped the ball as a leader?
- What behaviours am I tolerating that I shouldn't?
- What feedback have I ignored or avoided?

It's not about blame- it's about ownership.

"Your culture is a reflection of what you've created, allowed, or ignored."

How to Begin the Culture Detox
So, what do you actually do when things feel broken? You begin again.

Start with a reset. Gather your team, however small. Speak openly about what you've noticed. Be honest about what's not working, and share your commitment to fixing it. Set new expectations. Revisit roles and responsibilities. Bring everyone back to the same page. Get to a position where you know how everyone is feeling about the situation and you can move forward and make decisions with that knowledge rather than guessing.

Next, rebuild communication. And no, that doesn't mean more meetings. It means better conversations. Schedule weekly check-ins - not just to talk about performance, but to see how people are really doing. Create opportunities for anonymous feedback. Document processes and job descriptions so people aren't constantly guessing. And most importantly, make space for one-to-one chats that feel supportive, not just evaluative.

When conflict arises (and it will), meet it head-on. Don't let discomfort become avoidance. If you're unsure how to navigate it, get help. A neutral third party - a coach, a mediator, even a wise friend - can make all the difference. This is not a place for your AI chatbot. The bias and lack of contextual understanding and human nuances are far too great - we are dealing with humans here not robots.

And don't forget the fun stuff: recognition, celebration, small wins. They matter. People want to feel seen.
They want to know their work means something. A moment of gratitude can restore morale faster than you think.

Finally, lead with transparency. If you mess up, own it. If you change direction, explain why. If things are hard, say so. You're not a machine. Your team doesn't expect perfection. But they do want honesty.

Steps to Detoxify Your Culture

1. Reset Expectations

Have a team meeting. Be honest about what's not working. Clarify roles, responsibilities, and what's changing.

2. Improve Communication

- Weekly check-ins
- Anonymous surveys or feedback tools
- Clear documentation of processes
- One-to-one catchups that aren't just performance reviews

3. Address Conflict Head-On

Have the hard conversations. Bring in a coach or mediator if needed. Don't let wounds fester.

4. Celebrate Wins

Make recognition a weekly habit. Acknowledge effort. Share progress. Celebrate growth.

5. Lead With Transparency

Admit mistakes. Explain decisions. Involve the team in problem-solving.

Small Team, Big Emotions

Here's the thing about small teams: the highs are higher, but the lows cut deeper.

So remember, when it's just you and a couple of others, every mood matters. Every comment echoes louder. Every win feels like a shared triumph. But every tension hangs heavier too.

This is why culture matters more - not less - in tiny businesses. If one person's energy is off, it affects everyone. If trust erodes, there's nowhere to hide. But the flip side is beautiful too. A healthy, connected, energised team can move mountains. And they'll want to - because they're in it with you.

Even if you're just working with a VA or a few freelancers, the way you interact with them sets the tone. Kindness, clarity, curiosity - these aren't fluff. They're foundations.

Treat small culture with big importance.

When to Let People Go (Even If It Hurts)

Sometimes, despite your best efforts, someone simply isn't a fit.

They might be great at the job but toxic to the team. Or resistant to feedback. Or just not aligned with where you're heading. Maybe your business is shrinking, and you can't afford the extra pair of hands anymore. And it is a fact that some things can be handled by introducing AI into the mix.

Letting someone go is never easy. It's human. It hurts. But it's often the bravest, kindest decision you can make - for you, for them, and for everyone else still showing up.

Do it with compassion. Be direct, but warm. Leave the door open to dignity. And when it's done, give yourself time to process. Firing someone doesn't make you heartless. Avoiding it when it's necessary? That's what erodes trust.

The only path forward is to let someone go:

- If they're undermining the team
- If they refuse to take feedback
- If they consistently create tension
- If your business is shrinking and you can't afford the cost

It's painful. But it's sometimes necessary.

Do it with compassion. Do it with integrity. But do it.

Rebuilding: Culture as a Strategic Asset

Culture isn't just a feel-good topic. It's a **strategic advantage**.

Once the air has cleared, something amazing happens. You start to rebuild - deliberately, wisely, joyfully.

And what you create? It won't just feel better. It'll 'work' better. A healthy culture is a competitive edge. It retains great people way more than the fancy pool table or coffee machine will. It attracts new ones. It reduces drama, sharpens focus, and makes your life infinitely more enjoyable.

Ask yourself:
- What do we stand for?
- How do we act when things are tough?
- What do we celebrate?
- What won't we tolerate - ever?

Write it down. Talk about it. Make it real. Your culture isn't an accessory. It's the heart of your business.

Checklist: Culture Health Check

- ☐ Roles and responsibilities are clear
- ☐ Feedback flows both ways
- ☐ Wins are regularly recognised
- ☐ Conflict is addressed early

- ☐ Leadership is consistent and transparent
- ☐ People feel safe to speak up

If you're unsure about those answers, don't panic. Noticing where the issues might be is where the work begins.

Because here's the truth: healthy businesses are built on healthy relationships. And culture? It's not a nice-to-have. It's non-negotiable. So take a breath. Take responsibility. And then take the first step toward something better.

You've got this.

Interlude - What they Wish You Knew...The Hidden Architecture

Advice from Emma-Jayne Broadway, Founder & CEO, Talent Partnership Consulting

What I wish more founders knew is this: your company won't fall apart because of one bad quarter, but it can unravel because of one unchecked people issue.

The product can be brilliant, the strategy sound. Yet time and again, I've seen startups stall or collapse because the human architecture wasn't solid. A co-founder quietly disengages. A high performer shutting down. A new hire who never really fitted. These aren't small glitches - they are early warnings that your structure is under strain.

Culture is the foundation slab.
Culture isn't about the company vision or your slogans. It's about how decisions are made, how people behave under pressure, and what is - and isn't - tolerated. If you don't define it early, a culture will emerge anyway. And it may not be the one you want.

Every hire shifts the frame.
Think of each person as a structural beam. Get it right and the whole frame strengthens. Get it wrong and you'll spend months trying to straighten things back up. Hiring isn't about filling a gap, it's about ensuring someone can thrive in your environment, share your values in practice (not just words), and do their best work with you.

Safety makes you stronger.
If your people don't feel safe to speak up, you'll never hear what you most need to know. Founders often think they're approachable, but psychological safety isn't assumed, it's built.

Invite dissent. Thank people for telling you uncomfortable truths. Model vulnerability yourself. That's how trust takes root.

Bringing in help is reinforcement, not failure.
We see too many founders hold on to broken dynamics because they fear the fallout of acting. But keeping someone in a role where they're struggling isn't kindness, it's avoidance. And it chips away at your credibility. Advisors, coaches, legal guidance, these aren't luxuries. They're reinforcements. Smart builders don't wait until the walls start shaking to call in help.

Here's the hardest truth: you cannot hold every beam in place on your own. Control feels protective, but it often hides cracks until they're too wide to ignore. The strongest founders are those who know when to let go.

Your product won't carry your vision forward. Your people will.

Protect the foundation, strengthen the frame, and scaling becomes so much easier.

Chapter 5

Compliance Blind Spots - Legal & Regulatory Oversights

The Cost of What You Don't Know

When we think about why small businesses fail, our minds tend to go straight to the obvious: cash flow issues, not enough sales, maybe a bit of founder burnout sprinkled on top. Money problems and market missteps. But tucked behind those well-known culprits is a quieter, sneakier risk - one that rarely makes it into the inspirational startup podcasts or glossy Instagram posts.

That risk? Compliance failure: missed filings, unregistered licenses, IP or trademark breaches, incorrect employment practices, or simply not understanding your obligations as a UK business owner.

Now, I know what you're thinking: "I'm too small for that to matter," or "That's something I'll worry about when I'm bigger." But let me gently wave a red flag here - compliance isn't just for big corporations with legal departments and risk assessments. It's for you too. Yes, you with the Etsy shop, or the one-woman consultancy, the cake business or the social enterprise still run from your kitchen table.

Because here's the thing about legal and regulatory oversight: it's like a pothole you didn't see coming. You can be driving along at full speed - growing your audience, shipping products, landing clients - and then one misstep (a missed tax filing, an expired license, an overlooked insurance policy or regulation requirement) can send everything crashing down. Sometimes dramatically. Often, expensively.

This chapter isn't here to panic you. It's here to shine a light on what often gets ignored - not because it's boring (although yes, parts of it are) - but because no one teaches this stuff unless you go looking for it. And by the time you need to know it, it might be too late. We'll unpack the hidden risks around legal and regulatory oversight that too many founders either ignore, delay, or don't even know exist - and what to do to make sure your business isn't vulnerable to penalties, forced closure, or even personal liability.

So let's talk about what compliance actually means, where the common blind spots lie, and how to build simple habits that keep your business safe without sending you into a panic spiral every time you get a letter from HMRC.

We'll unpack the hidden risks around legal and regulatory oversight that too many founders either ignore, delay, or don't even know exist - and what to do to make sure your business isn't vulnerable to penalties, forced closure, or even personal liability.

What Does "Compliance" Really Mean?

Let's break it down.

Compliance simply means doing the things you're legally supposed to do as a business owner. Not just the headline stuff like paying your taxes, but the less glamorous, easily-forgotten details like renewing your public liability insurance, compliance with health and safety rules, not copying someone else's logo, filing a confirmation statement with Companies House, or registering with the ICO if you collect email addresses.

Compliance includes:

- Choosing the right business structure (sole trader? limited company?)
- Filing the right reports to the right people at the right times

- Understanding employment law if you hire people (yes, even part-timers or freelancers)
- Meeting tax deadlines and registering for VAT when you need to
- Following GDPR rules when you collect and store customer data
- Carrying the right insurance for what you do
- Staying within the line with industry-specific regulations (like health and safety or professional conduct)

Basically, it's the paperwork part of running a business. And while it might not be exciting, it's essential.

"I thought I didn't need to register for VAT because I was just freelancing. Turns out I crossed the threshold six months earlier - and ended up with a fine and a headache."

- A very stressed-out web designer I once met over coffee

And it doesn't matter if you're a sole trader, limited company, or side hustler - **you're still responsible** for meeting those obligations.

The Most Common Compliance Blind Spots (and why they matter)

Let's run through the places where founders most often trip up - to help you avoid that "Why didn't anyone tell me?!" moment down the line.

1. Annual Filings with Companies House

If you're running a limited company, there are annual filings you can't afford to forget. These include:

- Annual accounts (even if you made no money)
- Confirmation statements (annually to check and confirm your company info)
- Director updates
- Shareholder and "persons with significant control" details

Miss them, and you could face fines. Keep missing them? Your company could be struck off the register - yes, actually dissolved, even if you are making money in your business and have potential to be a success.

And no, they don't accept "I was busy" as a valid excuse.

2. Tax Registration and Reporting

Whether you're a sole trader or a limited company, you need to get on top of your tax responsibilities:

- Sole traders: Register for Self Assessment and submit your returns annually.
- Limited companies: Register for Corporation Tax and file annual accounts and CT600 forms.
- VAT: If your turnover crosses £85,000 (2025) in any 12-month period, you need to register.
- PAYE: If you're employing staff (even just paying yourself through payroll), you need to register for Pay As You Earn.

Late filings lead to penalties. Incorrect filings can trigger audits, interest charges, and some pretty uncomfortable letters from HMRC.

3. Employment Law Oversights

Thinking of hiring your first team member? Great! But make sure you:

- Set up payroll properly (and report through Real Time Information)
- Provide a legally sound employment contract
- Enrol them into a workplace pension scheme if they qualify
- Have employer's liability insurance
- Understand rules around holiday, maternity pay, sick pay, and grievance procedures

Even small mistakes can open you up to tribunal claims - and they don't just cost money. They cost time, energy, and reputation.

4. GDPR and Data Protection (Yes, still a thing)

If you're storing client details, sending emails, or using cookies on your website, you're handling personal data - and that means you have responsibilities.

You need to:

- Have a clear privacy policy
- Gain proper consent to use people's data (no sneaky pre-ticked boxes)
- Register with the ICO - the Information Commissioners Office (yes, even if you're tiny)
- Handle Subject Access Requests properly
- Remove people who ask to be removed from any lists you have on or off line

GDPR isn't just for tech giants. Many a small business has been fined thousands for a cookie consent error. You don't want to be the next example in a legal webinar.

5. Insurance Gaps

What insurance do you need? It depends on what you do. But here are the basics:

- Public liability (if people interact with you physically)
- Professional indemnity (for consultants, coaches, or anyone offering advice)
- Product liability (if you sell physical goods)
- Cyber liability (if you store client data digitally)

Often, people skip this because "nothing's gone wrong yet." But insurance isn't for when things go right.

How Blind Spots Create Business Risk

It's easy to think the worst that can happen is a fine. But compliance slip-ups can do far more damage than that. Compliance issues can:

- Freeze your bank account (yes really!)
- Cancel your contracts or prevent you from winning them
- Prevent investment approval at the last hurdle
- Kill your chances of getting a grant or loan
- Stop Corporates from working with you
- Void your insurance
- Trigger HMRC investigations
- Damage trust with customers and partners
- Lead to a public tribunal, court action or forced closure
- Result in personal liability as a Director

> **"We lost an £18k contract because our data policy was out of date. One quick update could've saved the whole deal."**
> - **Small agency founder, still fuming**

Why Founders Often Miss This Stuff

Let's be honest- this isn't anyone's favourite part of the job. But here's why it gets overlooked:

1. Overwhelm

When you're juggling sales, client work, marketing, admin, and trying to eat lunch, legal tasks fall to the bottom of the pile.

2. Misinformation

There's a lot of "bro advice" out there. "You don't need to register for tax until you hit £1 million" ....is not a thing.

3. False Simplicity

Many sole traders or side hustlers assume these rules don't apply to them. But they do. The scale of your business doesn't change the rules - it just changes the paperwork.

4. Trying to Save Money

Skipping legal advice or an accountant might seem frugal at first. But the cost of cleaning up a compliance mess is always more expensive. And yes you can get insight from AI to help you work out what you need, but when it comes to actual legal paperwork - get a professional involved.

What Compliance Looks Like at Each Stage

Let's demystify what you actually need to do- and when.

Early Stage

- Register with HMRC or Companies House
- Get your UTR and set up Self Assessment
- Basic public liability insurance (especially if seeing clients face-to-face)
- Privacy policy and cookie consent if you have a website (this you can create with AI)

Growth Stage

- Set up payroll (even if it's just for you)
- Get on top of VAT if you cross the threshold
- Write up staff or freelancer contracts
- Register with the ICO
- Sort pensions
- Set up employer and director insurances

Established Stage

- Run regular compliance checks
- Review contracts annually
- Keep IP and trademarks up to date
- Understand new laws if expanding overseas or into new industries

Where to Get Help (Without Breaking the Bank)

You don't have to do it all yourself, and AI can help a lot in the prep of these elements especially if you do a good job of setting your business context - but you don't need a team of lawyers either. You do however need some professionals in the mix.

1. A Good Accountant

They can help with:

- Tax registration
- VAT thresholds
- PAYE setup
- Cash flow aligned with tax deadlines

Choose one who understands small business, ask your friends or small business networks, make sure they aren't one that does just year-end accounts.

2. Affordable Legal Templates (Done Properly)

Use trusted platforms like:

- *LawBite*
- *Farillio*
- *Rocket Lawyer UK*...for affordable contracts and employment docs
- *SeedLegals*....to get investment over the line fast, and expanding now into other areas

Make sure the templates are UK specific and updated regularly.

3. Government Guidance

- *GOV.UK*: For all official business obligations - Companies House, employment, and tax info
- *ICO.org.uk*: For data guidance
- *FSB*, *IPSE*, and *Enterprise Nation*: Provide templates, advice, and hotlines for support

4. Industry Bodies

If your work is regulated (like fitness, food, therapy, or education), your trade association likely has industry-specific compliance checklists and updates.

Checklist: Are You Legally Compliant?

- ☐ I've registered the correct business structure
- ☐ I file accounts and tax returns on time
- ☐ I hold valid insurance for what I do
- ☐ I know I have not breached anyone's IP or trademarks
- ☐ I've registered with the ICO (if handling data)
- ☐ I use up-to-date contracts with staff/freelancers and clients
- ☐ I know my VAT threshold and reporting obligations
- ☐ I've documented processes and policies for health, safety, and complaints
- ☐ I've reviewed my legal set up in the last 12 months

If you can't tick at least six of these, it's time for a compliance review. In reality you should have all of these ticked to be confident that you won't get tripped up in future.

Simple Habits That Prevent Big Problems

- Set **calendar reminders** for key filing dates
- Create a **compliance folder** (Google Drive, Dropbox, or a digital or even a notebook or folder with everything printed out)
- Schedule an **annual review** to check compliance with your accountant or legal advisor
- Use a CRM (a database management programme) to track data handling consents

- Create a process for reviewing your contracts and policies each year - perhaps that first week in January or a day during Twixmas if you get really bored!
- Don't leave compliance to chance - it's not worth it

"When everything else in business feels hard, compliance feels impossible. But when you make it part of your rhythm, it stops being scary."

Final Thought: Compliance as Leadership

Being compliant doesn't make you boring. It makes you a grown-up founder. Someone who cares about protecting what they're building. Someone who's serious about trust, reputation, and resilience. It's not about ticking boxes. It's about maturity. Stability. Long-term thinking. And no, it won't get you thousands of likes. But it might save your business one day.

"Success leaves a trail. So does negligence. Don't let ignorance be what costs you everything.

Interlude - What They Wish You Knew...The Legal Basics Every Founder Should Tackle

Tips from Caroline Hughes - a commercial lawyer and co-founder of Hive Founders.

When you're building a startup, your mind is full of big ideas, user growth, and the next pitch meeting. Legal stuff? Often filed under "we'll deal with that later." And that's where trouble starts. Because ignoring legal foundations isn't just risky, it really can cost you your company.

First, let's talk about intellectual property (IP). Your software code, your designs, your logo, and your secret sauce are valuable. But if your employees, contractors, or advisors haven't signed agreements assigning IP to the company, technically, you might not own them. That brilliant feature or branding could legally belong to someone else. Make sure everyone who has been involved in creating something for your business has transferred the IP rights to you.

Next, contracts. Every relationship that your business has, with customers, suppliers, employees, advisors, needs clear agreements in place. The same is true for your shareholders. Most founders don't put a shareholder agreement in place until quite late in the day (often after they've raised VC investment). But a good shareholder agreement can protect you from co-founder disputes.

Then there's statutory compliance. Companies must file annual accounts, corporate filings, and taxes on time. Miss deadlines and you risk fines, penalties or your company being closed down. In some cases, directors or officers can be held personally liable. Have good systems and calendar reminders in place, so you never miss a filing.

Handling personal data is another area founders underestimate. Whether it's GDPR in Europe, CCPA in California, or other global rules, mishandling customer or employee data can lead to big fines, reputational damage, and regulatory scrutiny. Know your obligations, store data responsibly, and make privacy a routine part of operations.

If you're thinking about fundraising, now is the time to get your house in order. Investors will ask for due diligence: IP assignments, contracts, corporate and financial documents. Startups with clean records and solid documentation sail through. Messy, incomplete records raise red flags and kill deals.

Finally, get a good startup lawyer. One who understands fast-growing, early-stage businesses in your sector. You need a lawyer that can help you with employment law, investment raising, and commercial contracts.

Tackle these issues early - contracts, IP, filings, data, and advisors - and you'll avoid costly legal surprises later..

Chapter 6

Pressure Cooker

When the Business Is No Longer Just Yours - The Emotional Landscape of Investment

Running a business is never simple. It's a daily dance between big dreams and hard realities, and even when you're calling the shots, you're never completely free from pressure. But when you introduce external funding - whether that's from angel investors, friends and family, or formal institutions - the stakes change. Suddenly, it's not just your dream on the line. It's someone else's money, belief, and trust riding on your every move.

This section of the book explores the emotional and strategic complexities of running a business that is not solely yours. As support systems go, investment or funding in the form of grants can accelerate progress and provide a sense of validation. But when things become difficult, the obligation to keep going, or the presence of investors, or money owed to friends can also intensify the pressure, complicate decision-making, and add layers of emotional weight.

This chapter is all about that shift - when your business becomes a shared venture, and what that means emotionally, strategically, and practically. I cover the weight of grant funding in the next chapter. While the mechanics of Investment and grants differ, the emotional weight of both can be just as heavy.

Should You Take Investment at All?

Not every founder reading this chapter will have already taken investment. Some of you might be here wondering whether it's the right move for you at all.

Maybe things are wobbling, and you're considering taking on external capital to stay afloat or take your product to the next stage.

But the thought of handing over a share of *your* business- or inviting other voices into your decision-making - makes your stomach churn. I understand that feeling completely.

Taking investment is not a sign of weakness. It's not a failure to go it alone. In fact, it can be the most strategic and resilient thing you do. But it must be a choice, not a panic button. The truth is that investors can sniff out a panicked founder running on fumes and no matter how glossy your deck, unless you can show your business has traction and you have what it takes to create a return on investment no amount of time put into trying to get investment will actually generate any money.

Here are a few things to ask yourself before stepping into the investor world:

- **Is your challenge purely financial?**
  If you've got product-market fit, strong demand, and a clear growth plan - but you just don't have the capital to meet that demand - investment could be the missing puzzle piece. If you are just panicking about not having the funds to run your business then it is the other chapters of this book you need to focus on.
- **Are you emotionally ready to share the reins?**
  Investment comes with accountability. Are you ready to be answerable to someone else about your decisions, timelines, and outcomes?
- **Do you know what kind of investor you need?**
  Not all money is equal. Some investors bring expertise and connections. Others bring pressure and chaos. You need to be as selective as they are.

This is really hard when you can see an end to your runway approaching but if that's the case choose smaller planes, corporate investment partners or angels who align with your business well.

- **What are you willing to give up- and what are your red lines?**
  You might need to offer equity, decision-making input, or a board seat. Know your boundaries before the first conversation.

If you are thinking investment is the answer to your prayers and will keep you alive, it isn't and it won't. That is not the frame of mind to approach investment with.

And on the flip side of that, if your resistance to investment is mostly about pride, independence, or fear of conflict - just pause. There are many ways to structure deals that still protect your vision. In fact, many investors respect and appreciate founders who are cautious, principled, and prepared.

So don't rule it out just because it feels uncomfortable. But don't leap into it just because you're desperate. Get clear first. Then decide.

Let's deal with the Investors first

While founders often experience personal and financial strain, bringing in investors - whether friends, family, or professional partners - adds accountability, responsibility, and, often, a fear of letting others down. You are not just risking your own resources. You are using other people's money, time, belief and trust.

When you bring investors into the mix, especially those you know personally, the emotional stakes shoot up. It's one thing to lose your own money. It's another thing entirely to feel like you might lose someone else's.

That's where guilt creeps in, followed closely by shame, panic, and a desperate need to prove that everything is still fine, even if it's not.

I've been there. I've stood in front of investors pretending confidence while internally, I was coming apart. I've held meetings after sleepless nights, trying to sound upbeat about a roadmap I wasn't sure we could afford to follow, with a promise that a product was due to release but knowing my CTO had told me we are nearly ready more times than I could count. The emotional impact of investment goes far beyond contracts - it sits in your chest, in your gut, and follows you into every conversation you have.

If you have never taken investment then as I've said at the start of this chapter, this might be an option you are considering, and it can often be a solution to cashflow issues, where all the other stars align around a galaxy of team, product, market need and demand, and it is genuinely just the money to fund stock or grow a team to cope with sales, that is driving you to look for investment. But whether you are here, before you take investment, or afterwards and you are now dealing with the aftermath of that not going well, there are some critical things to know and factor in for both positions.

The emotional landscape becomes more complex. Disappointment isn't just self-contained. It's shared. You begin to worry not only about the future of the business, but about the future of relationships.

When someone invests in your business, there's often a subtle but important shift in how decisions are made and justified.

Whether they're passive shareholders or active board members, investors tend to expect transparency, performance, and returns.

Even the most laid-back funder is still, on some level, assessing whether you're making the right calls.

Here's how the emotional landscape often shifts:

- **Fear-based decision-making** - You stop choosing what's best and start choosing what's safest.
- **Avoidance of transparency** - You put off sharing bad news.
- **Performative optimism** - You keep the mask on, even when you're out of breath.
- **Founder burnout** - You carry the load of performance, hope, and reputation.

Even when your investors are kind, supportive, or seemingly uninvolved, you'll still likely feel the pressure. Because whether it's a friend who loaned you money or an angel fund who took a punt on your vision, it *matters* that you deliver.

Even when investment contracts are clear, the emotional impact can remain unspoken. Founders often report feeling:

- Guilt, when milestones are missed
- Shame, if the business underperforms
- Isolation, because they can't be transparent with their team
- Paralysis, when next steps are unclear and pressure mounts

You may also experience "performative optimism," where you continue to act confident and positive in updates and meetings - even when internally, you're falling apart.

The Many Faces of Investors

Friends and Family: This group is the most emotionally loaded. If it goes badly, it's not just about missed returns. It's birthdays, Christmases, and future barbecues wrapped up in awkward silences and unspoken disappointments.

Angel Investors: Often well-meaning and full of entrepreneurial empathy - but don't mistake their kindness for a lack of expectation. They still want results.

Institutional Funders: Here come the formalities - board reports, KPIs, structured updates. You might find yourself justifying every decision to a spreadsheet.

Crowdfunders: Possibly the most vocal group. Hundreds (or thousands) of people have backed you based on your story. Now they want to know how the next chapter ends. Preferably with a happy ever after.

If performance starts to dip or things veer off course (and trust me, they will at some point), how you communicate matters:

1. **Own the Reality Early**: Avoiding bad news only delays trust erosion.
2. **Explain the Why**: Context is everything.
3. **Offer Next Steps**: Even if you're not sure of the outcome, show you have a plan.
4. **Stay Honest, Not Catastrophic**: Panic doesn't help. But neither does pretending it's all fine.
5. **Stay Human**: Investors are human too. When you speak with humility and clarity, most will respond in kind.

Key Pressures Investors Can Bring to Bear on Startups

1. Clauses That Undermine Founder Autonomy

Unfortunately, when times are tough, I have been so desperate to get investment in, that I haven't fully paid attention to the clauses that an investor might have slipped into an investment agreement, or really understood the implications of what is there....until they came back to bite me. So I am going to spell these out here so you know what to look for.

Examples of **Restrictive** Clauses:

- **Control Rights**: Investors demand board seats or majority voting rights, limiting founders' ability to make decisions without approval.
- **Liquidation Preferences**: Investors secure returns that prioritize their interests (e.g., 2x or 3x liquidation preference), leaving founders and other stakeholders with little in case of a sale or liquidation.
- **Veto Power**: Investors may require veto power over key business decisions, such as additional fundraising, hiring executives, or changing the company's strategy.

Risks to the Business:

- Decision-making slows to a crawl.
- Your vision gets diluted.
- You feel like a CEO in name only.

How to Navigate:

- **Get legal advice**. No excuses. This is not a place to save money but there are great digital services out there that can help.

- **Negotiate Carefully**: Seek legal advice before signing any term sheets or agreements. Push for clauses that retain founder autonomy, such as shared decision-making rather than investor veto power.
- **Limit Voting Rights**: Ensure investors do not hold disproportionate voting power relative to their equity stake.
- **Cap Liquidation Preferences**: Negotiate reasonable caps on investor preferences to avoid founders being left with little in the event of an exit.
- **Research:** how much to give away at each stage, and what milestones and expectations align with Pre-seed/Seed and subsequent rounds - this varies by country and changes according to the economic climate so check what is normal now

2. Pressures to Scale Prematurely

Investor Push:

Investors often want to see rapid growth to increase valuation, even when the business isn't ready (e.g., launching into new markets or using precious budget on over-hiring).

Risks to the Business:

Sometimes investors want you to scale when you are still building the engine. To me it felt like being pushed off a cliff while I was still making my own parachute. Scaling too quickly can lead to operational inefficiencies, cash flow problems, and diluted focus on the core product or service. It burns through cash, which ironically is what the investors want you to do. But if you don't meet the milestones they want you to reach, within the timeline they have set for reporting profits and growth and returns on investment to their own Boards and Investors (yes they have them too) then they won't continue to invest leaving you high and dry with no cash. And you are vulnerable to being sold in a fire sale just so the investors can recover their cash.

Premature expansion also risks alienating early customers due to a drop in quality or service. So you are stuck. No customers, no investment, no cash to continue.

I found I had a small group of investors who wanted us to rapidly bring on clients with a product that didn't work, to push us to a point where the business looked good enough to be sold rather than realise it's full potential. They had come in on a down round with a very low valuation on the business when we were trying to keep going after my ex co-founder upped and left. I hadn't realised they were just out to make a fast buck on their low price shares and weren't really committing to helping the business grow. They announced they wanted to sell their shares right in the middle of my next fully priced round six months after becoming investors. It was a much higher value Pre-Seed round, with a higher share price for any new incoming investors that they thought they might benefit from.

What were they doing? Totally risking the round for themselves. Yes. Their strategy all along. Probably.

We managed it but it was tough, negotiating for existing shareholders to buy at a lower price, and offering new investors a few of the lower priced shares as a portion of their shareholding, so the selling investors had a small upside and other shareholders were able to buy their shares at a less than valuation price.

Pushing a business to try and create an illusion of success in order to sell it is a common Investor tactic. Not capitulating to this demand meant a complete nightmare from the time it took to managing perceptions during an already challenging investment round.

Whether you give in to the pressure to scale or you don't the risks are the same:

- Burnout.
- Operational chaos.
- Customers leave due to poor service.

How to Navigate:

- **Set Realistic Milestones**: Communicate clear, achievable goals to investors, backed by data and timelines.
- **Push Back Strategically**: Show evidence of why slower, more sustainable growth is better in the long run.
- **Protect the Core**: Prioritize customer satisfaction and product-market fit over aggressive growth metrics.

3. Conflicting Objectives: Founder vs. Investor

Typical Conflicts:

- **Short-Term ROI vs. Long-Term Vision**: Similar to above, investors may prioritize quick returns, while founders may want to invest in sustainable growth.
- **Exit Pressure**: Investors may push for a sale or IPO to realize their returns, even if the business isn't ready or this doesn't align with the founder's vision.
- **Cost Cutting vs. Innovation**: Investors might demand reduced spending, which could stifle product development and innovation.

Risks to the Business:

- You feel torn and pressured into decisions that compromise the long-term health of the company.
- Everyone gets frustrated as strategic disagreements damage morale and slow progress.

How to Navigate:

- **Vet investors and Align Early:** During fundraising, seek investors who share your vision and priorities. Screen for alignment during the pitch process.
- **Build Relationships**: Maintain open and transparent communication with investors to build trust and reduce conflict.
- **Use Advisory Boards**: Create a buffer between founders and investors by involving neutral advisors who can mediate conflicts and offer objective guidance.

4. Pre-Pack Administration Manipulation

Pre-pack administration sounds tidy. Quick. Painless even. But when it's used to wrest control from the founder, it's brutal.

It's among the more talked-about - and sometimes side-eyed - options for business restructuring. It sounds a bit like something you'd grab off a supermarket shelf in a rush ("pre-packed and ready to go!"), and in some ways, that's not far off. But here also was my final downfall in my last business which on the outside seemed to have much going for it...in reality we were circling the drain.   Investors floated a pre-pack - but not to save the business. To buy it. Themselves. Cheap. It felt like betrayal.

And the impact? I felt I had no choice but to walk away from the business that I had spent years building and which was my only source of income.

A pre-pack is essentially a behind-the-scenes arrangement where the business is sold - often to existing directors or a connected party - before it even formally enters administration. The moment the administrator is appointed, the sale goes through, quick as a flash. The idea is to preserve the value of the business by avoiding the drawn-out chaos that public insolvency processes can bring.

Done well, it can protect jobs, keep the lights on, and ensure some sort of continuity. But it's not without its controversies. Creditors, in particular, can feel blindsided, since they often hear about the deal *after* it's already been done - a bit like being told the party's over just as you arrive with your bottle of wine. For all its stealth and speed, the pre-pack is still a form of administration - just with the rescue plan neatly tucked under the administrator's arm before they've even walked through the door.

Investor Push:

A Prepack is a great option if the circumstances are right, and can bring a new lease of life to a business that is otherwise stifled from growing, and I explore this more in Chapter 11 where I go through the alternatives for closing down a business - but in challenging times, investors may pressure the founder into a pre-pack sale, where the business is sold (often to the investor themselves) at a fraction of its value.

Risks to the Business:

- You lose the business. Investors acquire it, leaving founders and employees with little to no compensation.
- They keep the brand, IP, and customers.

How to Navigate:

Understand Pre-Pack Dynamics: A pre-pack can save the business but must be handled transparently. Retain an independent advisor to ensure the process is fair. Remember it costs money to do this.

Retain Legal Support: Ensure contracts with investors in the first place either right at the beginning when they first invest, or if you are planning this, include protections against them forcing a pre-pack for personal gain.

Explore Alternatives: Before agreeing to a pre-pack, consider restructuring, negotiating with creditors, or seeking bridge funding.

5. Excessive Focus on Financial Metrics

Investor Push:

Investors may fixate on specific metrics (e.g., Monthly Recurring Revenue, burn rate, or CAC/LTV ratios) without considering the business's broader context. But remember you know your business and a big part of this is reigning in your dream and ambition when sharing it in the first place. Yes it gets investors excited, but those projections you shared in that deck.

Well those are the ones your progress will be measured by. The projections you dazzle them with now will be the stick you're measured by later.

And I have learnt it is better to overdeliver than under when it comes to investors.

Risks to the Business:

- Operational decisions to try and meet targets may prioritize short-term metrics over long-term strategy.
- Product quality, customer experience, or innovation may suffer to meet arbitrary financial goals and milestones.

How to Navigate:

Educate Investors: Share the bigger picture and the steps you're taking to balance short-term performance with long-term goals.

Regular Updates: Use detailed, transparent investor updates to show how key metrics align with strategic progress. Data + context = reassurance.

6. Risk of Investor-Led Takeovers

Investor Push:

Own too little and you may not own your future. If investors hold a majority stake or control critical decisions, they can force founders out of their roles or even acquire the business outright. Make sure you understand how the dilution of your shareholding reduces for each round now, and forecast how it will reduce in the future.

Risks to the Business:

- Founders lose control and potentially their jobs.
- The business may pivot in a direction that alienates early customers or employees.

How to Navigate:

Protect Equity: During funding rounds, avoid giving up too much ownership or control, even if it means raising less capital. There is plenty of info out there regarding what to expect to give away each round but it should never be more than 20% per round and the founder should still have control (i.e. over 50% of shares in the business, and voting rights over up to 80% of the shareholding base if possible) until Series A.

Include your own Protective Clauses: Negotiate contracts that prevent investors from unilaterally taking control, with mechanisms such as non-dilution clauses or founder veto rights.

Be Cautious with Board Seats: You need independent and effective oversight at Board level.

Limit the number of board seats allocated to investors, who have an agenda that is not always visible, and ensure an independent chairperson.

Broader Risks Founders Should Be Aware Of

1. Down Rounds and Dilution

What Happens: If a startup raises a new round at a lower valuation than before, founders may experience significant dilution of their equity. Especially if the investor has a clause protecting them from down rounds so their share proportion basically increases, or stays the same but when the business is eventually sold, the value/price of their shares is much higher than your shares. Basically diluting you even further on the financial return.

Mitigation: Avoid over-inflating valuations early. Keep funding rounds tied to measurable milestones.

2. Pressure to Overpromise

What Happens: Early Investors may push founders to make unrealistic (disguised as ambitious) projections during pitches or funding rounds and you agree to go along with it to get the investment. But the outcome is you have to achieve those results or you are positioning the business to be undervalued later based on poor performance against the targets you said you could achieve. Remember what I said about dazzling early investors with your projections at the start, because it will turn into the stick they beat you with ... .turns out those investors will do the very same to others as well.

Mitigation: Focus on achievable, data-backed forecasts to maintain credibility.

3. Investor Fatigue

What Happens: Investors may lose patience (or simply get bored) if the business doesn't meet milestones or requires repeated funding without showing results.

Mitigation: Keep investors engaged with clear updates, celebrate wins, and demonstrate strategic progress.

Navigating investor pressures is one of the most challenging aspects of running a startup.

You have to balance satisfying investors with maintaining the integrity and vision of your business. By negotiating smart contracts, aligning with the right investors, and protecting decision-making autonomy, founders can reduce risks and build stronger relationships with their backers.

Red Flags to Watch for in Investor Relationships

Investors, well-meaning or otherwise, can bring a specific kind of pressure that distorts your decisions. Some of these are obvious, but many sneak in subtly, wrapped in well-intentioned WhatsApp messages.   Investor issues rarely arrive like thunderbolts. They show up quietly.

A comment here, a controlling clause there, a shift in tone on a Zoom call that you ignore because "it's probably nothing."

Let's talk about the most common warning signs- so you can act early rather than untangling a mess later.

1. Aggressive or Unreasonable Demands

When investors pressure you into decisions that feel out of step with your strategy- like pivoting too soon or hiring/firing based on their opinions- you may be dealing with misaligned goals.

2. Power Grabs

When voting rights, veto powers, or control of budgets start creeping beyond their equity share, you've got a governance problem.

3. Behind-the-Scenes Undermining

Investors having one-on-one conversations with your team without you, sowing doubt, or speaking negatively about your leadership? That's not mentorship. That's interference.

4. Inconsistency and Absenteeism

Investors who ghost you when things are going well but come roaring in when there's trouble are fair-weather partners. That pattern erodes trust quickly.

5. Prioritising Personal Gain

Pushing for sales, pre-packs, or restructuring that benefit them more than the business is a red flag waving wildly.

Exiting a Contentious Investor Situation

Sometimes, despite our best efforts and the rosiness of early pitch decks, investor relationships sour. It happens more often than people like to admit. What starts as a shared dream can turn into a tug-of-war over vision, money, control - or simply clashing personalities. And when that happens, you're left with a difficult but crucial decision: do I stick it out, or do I find a way to exit the relationship?

Why It's Critical to Address Investor Conflict Early

Tension doesn't usually vanish on its own. Left unaddressed, it festers. A simmering investor conflict can undermine your leadership, shake your team's confidence, and drain your time and emotional bandwidth. Getting ahead of the issue - before it unravels everything - is key.

Step 1: Understand the Root of the Conflict

What's really going wrong?

- Are expectations misaligned?
- Is one party trying to dominate decisions?
- Is the investor overly involved in day-to-day decisions?
- Has trust eroded because of missed targets or lack of transparency?
- Has the investor expressed dissatisfaction with your leadership or results?

Ask yourself:

Can this be resolved with better communication or mediation? Or is the investor's agenda now fundamentally incompatible with your vision?

Step 2. Conduct a Risk Analysis

Evaluate the potential consequences of maintaining the relationship versus exiting it.

Consider:

- **Financial impact:** Will their exit strain your resources or limit funding opportunities?
- **Reputational risks:** Could their departure harm your credibility with future investors or stakeholders?

Step 3: Check the Legal Groundwork

You need to know where you stand before making any moves.

- **Equity stakes and rights:** What percentage of the business do they own, and what voting power do they have?
- **Exit clauses:** Do the agreements specify conditions under which they or you can exit?
- **Control clauses:** Do they have veto power or specific rights over operational decisions?

Work with a corporate lawyer to review your options for ending the relationship. Understand the legal implications of actions such as buybacks, dilution, or seeking new investors to replace them.

Step 4: Explore Your Options

There are multiple ways to change the dynamic or exit entirely:

1. **Buy Back Their Shares**
   If you can raise the capital personally or one of your other shareholders is keen, this can reset control. It's expensive, although often the shares are at a reduced rate as they no longer have the attractive tax relief when they are sold second hand. It's a clean approach.

2. **Find a Replacement Investor**
   Someone you know? Skills you could use? Someone who knows you and likely understands that the departing investor wasn't a good fit. This brings in fresh energy and alignment. Just be sure to avoid repeating past mistakes.

3. **Dilution Through a New Funding Round**
   This reduces their influence - though it may sour the relationship further. But the reality is there is little an investor can do if your legal agreements give your Board, or you as a Director of the business the ability to create shares. Get legal advice, but if there is no clause saying you can't issue new shares then create them, issue them to the new investors or yourself and dilute the investor.

4. **Structured Sale or Pre-Pack Administration**
   Can offer continuity for the business, but as you know from my experience shared earlier, beware of being cut out.

5. **Legal Remedy**
   In much the same way that Directors have a responsibility to act in good faith within a business, If the investor has violated the terms of your agreement or

acted in bad faith, you may have grounds for legal action. Only use this route if there's clear misconduct. It's slow, costly, and rarely pleasant. Legal disputes can be time-consuming, expensive, and damaging to your reputation. And remember the investor probably has a lot more money and time than you do.

Step 5: Managing the Exit Process

- **Negotiate calmly and professionally.**
  Use facts, stay composed, and bring in a mediator if emotions are high. Remember you are in control. They remain a shareholder regardless and you are under no obligation to sell their shares for them, and they are unlikely to be able to sell them without you.
- **Safeguard your team and operations.**
  Hard, especially if you are a small team but try and shield the day to day from the drama. Maintain normalcy while changes are underway. Avoid sharing sensitive information including business updates, with the investor during this period unless legally required.
- **Be transparent with other stakeholders.**
  Share what's appropriate, with your team, and other shareholders. Do this with integrity and honesty - you may find experience you can use amongst your supporters and build confidence in your leadership.

Step 6: Rebuild and Reflect

- **Extract the learning.**
  What could have gone differently? Be honest.

- **Refine your investor criteria.**
  And update your agreements accordingly if you discovered areas were weak and let you as the founder

down when you needed the protection..

- **Use this moment to reignite your vision.**
  You may be bruised- but you're wiser and more resilient now.Reassure your team, customers, and stakeholders that the business is on track. Leverage the exit as an opportunity to recalibrate and refocus on your vision. Trust your gut next time!

Exiting a contentious relationship doesn't mean you've failed. It means you've chosen integrity over inertia. And who knows - some of your former investors might still back your next venture, simply because you handled the hard stuff with grace.

Taking on investment is a bold move. It says: I believe in this enough to let someone else in. To share the risk, the reward - and yes, the responsibility. It's empowering and terrifying all at once.

When it works, investment can be the rocket fuel that takes your business from a good idea to great impact. It can connect you to expertise, expand your network, and give your vision the resources it needs to breathe.

But when it doesn't work? It can feel like you've sold off pieces of your dream to people who don't see it the way you do. And when the business begins to struggle, those external pressures can make everything feel a thousand times heavier. You're no longer just dealing with your own disappointment. You're carrying the weight of theirs, too.

Still, if there's one thing I've learned, it's this: most of the harm doesn't come from the failure itself. It comes from the silence around it.

From the secrecy, the shame, the long nights pretending to be okay. From hiding the truth until it becomes too big to manage.

So whether your business is booming or buckling, communicate. Be honest. Stay human. Honour the people who've backed you - not with false confidence, but with thoughtful transparency.

And if you find yourself at the end of the road- if winding down is the only viable option- then offer closure, not avoidance:

- Prepare a final update - even if informal.
- Return any unspent funds, where applicable.
- Clarify liabilities, openly.
- Say thank you. Mean it.

You might be surprised, as I was, by how many investors respond with grace, encouragement, or even another offer to back you again. Maybe not today, but one day.

You may not be able to return their capital. But you can return their trust. And that, in the end, might be worth just as much.

Interlude - What They Wish You Knew... Fundraising 101

Contributed by David B Horne, the exceptionally knowledgeable Author of Add then Multiply and Funded Female Founders.

The title of this chapter, "The Pressure Cooker" sums it up well. Taking someone else's money to grow a business comes with responsibilities. Used well, it's one of the best accelerators to growth, because you are not constrained by your own resources and can take swift and decisive action to invest – whether taking on new staff, acquiring technology or other assets, or investing in marketing and sales.

The problem is that most entrepreneurs approach fundraising backwards. They wait until they desperately need money, throw together a pitch deck, and wonder why investors aren't queuing up to write cheques. And they fail to have experienced advisors before entering into a transaction. Over the course of my career, I have raised over £110 million from public markets, private equity, venture capital, angel investors, crowdfunding platforms and loans.

The biggest mistake entrepreneurs make is treating fundraising as a one-off event rather than a strategic process. I've watched brilliant businesses fail to secure funding simply because they approached it like a transaction instead of a relationship. Meanwhile, average businesses with better preparation secured millions. The difference isn't the quality of the business. It's the quality of the approach. When you understand that funding isn't about keeping the lights on but about accelerating exponential growth, everything changes.

Your pitch becomes more compelling, your negotiations more strategic, and your chances of success dramatically higher. I like to focus on three areas:

1. Intelligent Timing – the best time to raise money is when you don't desperately need it. Market conditions, investor sentiment, and your business metrics all affect success rates. Strategic fundraisers raise before they need to, not after.

2. Investor Alignment – different money comes with different expectations. Angel investors, VCs, and private equity all serve different purposes in your growth journey. Understanding which type fits your current stage prevents costly mismatches.

3. Preparation Excellence – investors don't fund ideas, they fund execution capability. Every element of your fundraising process should demonstrate competence, from financial modelling to market analysis to team readiness.

Once you have successfully raised money, the key lesson that every entrepreneur must learn is that it's not your business anymore. Ownership is shared, and with shared ownership comes shared responsibility. You must communicate with your investors, and communication is a two-way street.

Chapter 7

The Temptation of "Free" Grant Funding

A Blessing or a Slow Trap?

For pre-revenue businesses, especially those navigating the tricky waters of tech and innovation, grant funding often feels like a golden ticket. Non-dilutive, supportive, and even validating, it seems like the dream scenario: someone pays you to build your idea, and you don't have to give away a single share. But here's the catch - grants are rarely free. Not emotionally. Not strategically. And definitely not in terms of your time.

I know this landscape intimately. In the early days of my career, I was a funding consultant helping clients secure grants with great success. Later, grant funding moved to being something I turned to to generate income to build businesses and technologies that could move me from a 'spread too thin' consultant to a thriving entrepreneur with products that had a proven market, investment in their R&D and basically would make money without me...or so I thought.

At first, it made sense. Grants helped keep the lights on, paid salaries, and gave us the structure to develop genuinely interesting tech. But over time, I realised I had unintentionally swapped financial freedom for project dependency - and worse, we were building products that served the funders more than the market.

Investors generally love to see grants being given to startups as it goes some way to de-risking their investment and makes the change of real innovation in the product higher and more likely to produce the elusive unicorn - but it switches after a couple of years. Then it becomes a big fat negative.

The twist is that while grants can be valuable, their impact on sales efforts, R&D tax credit eligibility, and investor perception on progress towards revenue milestones must be carefully considered.

This was the issue. Time vapourisation. All the time spent on product development meant that I was less focused on sales. Or anything other than the funded project requirements. The money from grants kept our lights on. For the length of each R&D project it created a comfortable illusion that finally we had financial certainty. I almost forgot about the consultancy that had been building up my networks and reputation as an expert, or the first basic MVP version of a product and getting this version sold and out in the wild to generate some sales and prove to investors people wanted what we were building.

Whilst the R&D projects were projects we explored in my innovation consultancy, testing out a few ideas on the side with grant funding was a great idea to validate potential spin out businesses.

Eventually one of these ideas was so strong we shut down the consultancy and focussed all our efforts on the new technology product where we had proven demand and built a proof of concept. That's where we should have stopped with the grant funding.

It became a big mistake when we continued to apply for and win funding to keep moving the R&D forwards. It led us to become overly dependent on R&D grant and loan funding to develop a really great, but complex and essentially over-thought and over-developed frankenstein product.

The grant's requirement that we truly innovate in technology pushing the state of the art meant we were reliant on emerging tech, which we had to build.

We presented to the world as an industry nirvana, but the tech was never quite there enough for us to get it to market.

So let's unpack the upside, the risks, and the hidden emotional tolls of grant funding - and how to use them without losing your focus, your customers, or your momentum.

1. The Allure and Challenges of Grant Funding Why Pre-Revenue Startups Seek Grants

Non-dilutive funding: Grants don't require giving up equity, making them attractive compared to raising funds from investors.

Support for innovation: Grants often target R&D-heavy projects, aligning with the goals of many startups.

Cashflow relief: Grants can cover key expenses, such as salaries, prototyping, and testing.

Key Challenges of Grant Funding

- **Time-intensive process:** Writing applications, meeting compliance requirements, and managing reporting can drain resources. Believe me it can take 8 full days to write an InnovateUK grant application, AI is not a substitute but it can help, but even so that is a lot of time to commit when because AI has helped raise the quality of applications, the chance of winning funding in an InnovateUK grant competition in 2024 was an average of 4-5%.
- **Restrictions on usage:** Grants often come with stipulations about how the funds must be spent, limiting flexibility.
- **Delayed payments:** Reimbursement-based grants require the business to front costs, you can generally

claim back 3 months worth of costs after you have incurred them - so at the end of a 3 month period that you must fund yourself, which can strain cash flow.

2. The Impact on Sales and Market Validation

Risk: Shifting Focus Away from Revenue Generation

Challenge: Pre-revenue startups may divert their time and energy toward fulfilling grant obligations rather than generating sales or engaging with customers.

Example: A team focusing on grant deliverables (e.g., detailed research reports or technical milestones) may delay launching their MVP or acquiring beta customers.

Impact on the Business:

- Slower time to market as the team prioritizes R&D over customer acquisition.
- Missed opportunities to validate the product and build customer relationships, which are critical for early traction.

What to Do:

- **Allocate resources strategically:** Dedicate specific team members or consultants to handle grant management while the core team focuses on sales.
- **Use grants strategically:** Align grant-funded R&D with customer needs to ensure efforts contribute to product-market fit.
- **Ring fence a project:** Make sure that the project is an isolated element of your business and your product so you can continue to grow revenue outside of the funded project itself.

- **Treat any grant funding as a bonus;** not something the business is dependent on to survive.

3. R&D Tax Credit Implications

Here's a less obvious problem: grants can interfere with your R&D tax credits. If your grant is considered "notified state aid" (as many UK grants are), then the same R&D expenses can't be claimed under the more generous SME tax credit scheme

Example: A grant covering 50% of your R&D costs could disqualify those same costs from being claimed at the higher SME tax credit rate, pushing them into the less generous RDEC (Research and Development Expenditure Credit) scheme.

Impact on the Business:

- Lower financial returns from R&D tax credits, reducing overall funding for the business.
- Potential misunderstandings about tax implications leading to unexpected cash flow issues.

What to Do:

- **Seek professional advice:** Speak to an R&D tax credit specialist or accountant who knows this stuff inside out before applying for grants to fully understand the impact on tax claims.
- **Maximize efficiency:** Structure your projects to isolate projects and separate grant-funded and non-grant-funded activities, ensuring the latter will get the higher rate SME tax credits. Your accountant won't like it cause it is more work but you can split your tax credit claim into two.

4. Investor Perception Risks

While some investors see grant funding as validation of a company's innovation, others may interpret heavy reliance on grants as a lack of commercial viability or customer demand.

Example: Investors might question why the business is prioritizing R&D over generating revenue or why the market isn't funding the product development through sales or venture capital.

Impact on the Business:

- Difficulties attracting equity investment if investors perceive grants as a crutch.
- Reduced confidence in the company's ability to generate sustainable revenue streams.

What to Do:

- **Position grants as supplemental:** Emphasize to investors that grants support long-term innovation, not core operations.
- **Demonstrate traction:** Ensure grant activities are paired with clear evidence of market demand, such as pre-sales, customer interest, or letters of intent.

5. Funding compliance Risks and Administrative Burden

Grants sometimes come with extensive reporting, compliance, and audit requirements, which can distract from the core business and mean you are pouring your team into simply keeping track of the things you are supposed to report on to your funders.

Grant funding often brings a whole new workload: paperwork, audits, milestone reviews, monthly reports. As a founder, this can feel like doing a part-time job for an even more part-time income.

The Risk:

- You're drained, distracted, and distant from your team and customers.

What to Do:

- **Outsource where possible**: Bring in a grant consultant or dedicated admin support.
- **Choose lighter grants**: Not all grants are created equal. Sometimes, smaller pots come with far less red tape.

6. Strategic Ways to Leverage Grant Funding

a) Align Grants with Business Goals

- Use grants to fund projects that directly contribute to achieving product-market fit, such as developing features requested by early adopters.
- Avoid using grants for speculative research that doesn't align with your commercialization timeline.

b) Use Grants to De-Risk Innovation

- Leverage grants to fund high-risk, high-reward innovation projects that would otherwise strain your budget.
- Example: Use a grant to test a new technology or prototype without jeopardizing the core business.

c) Communicate Grant Benefits to Stakeholders

- To investors: Highlight how grant funding supplements, rather than replaces, commercial funding.
- To customers: Emphasize how grant-funded innovations improve your product or service offering.

Conclusion: Balance Is Key

Grant funding helped me test ideas, build connections, and experiment without financial risk. But I also learned the hard way what happens when you start building your business around the grants - not the market.

In the end, grants should help you build momentum, not replace it. Used well, they're a springboard. Used poorly, they're a slow, polite, bureaucratic distraction from what really matters.

So go ahead and apply. But stay focused. Know what the grant is really buying you - and never let it cost you your direction.

Chapter 8

The Founder Fog - Burnout, Fatigue and Isolation

Something has changed...

There's a kind of fatigue that isn't physical, though it lives in the body. A weariness that settles into your thoughts, colours your reactions, and starts to press gently but relentlessly against the edges of your personality. It's not obvious to anyone else - not at first. Your team may not notice. Your clients probably wouldn't guess. Your friends might assume you're just "busy again." But you know something has shifted.

You're still showing up. Still delivering. Still pushing forward. And yet, you've stopped feeling anything about it. It all feels flat.

This is the fog that descends on so many founders - the slow encroachment of burnout and disconnection that rarely announces itself in a single moment, but instead creeps in quietly through the cracks of overcommitment, emotional suppression, and chronic overwork. It doesn't usually arrive with a breakdown. It begins with small changes in tone, behaviour, and outlook. A hesitance to check your inbox. A hollow feeling during meetings. A short fuse with your loved ones. A sense of dread on Sunday night that never really fades, even on Friday evening.

In the early days of building a business, you're carried by energy- vision, adrenaline, momentum. You're fuelled by excitement, ideas, and the thrill of building something new. Every setback is a lesson. Every win, a validation. It's demanding, yes, but the effort feels worthwhile. It's aligned.

But over time, the cumulative strain starts to build. Not just the long hours or the financial pressure - though those matter too - but the emotional load of being the one who holds it all.

You are not only the decision-maker, the executor, the marketer, and the customer service rep. You are also the person who answers to yourself, who holds the vision, who absorbs the uncertainty. You are the safety net, the brand, the leader, and the system. The human machinery that makes everything run.

And eventually, that machinery begins to falter.

What makes this so difficult to recognise - especially for high-functioning, ambitious individuals- is that burnout at the founder level doesn't always look like collapse. It doesn't always look like someone curled up in bed unable to face the day. Sometimes, it looks like someone attending every meeting, replying to every email, shipping the work, ticking the boxes - and feeling absolutely nothing while doing it.

That numbness is insidious. It convinces you that maybe you're just in a rut. Maybe the work has become boring. Maybe you're growing out of the business. Or maybe this is just how it is. But underneath that narrative is a truth that many founders struggle to admit: you're running on empty, emotionally, mentally, and sometimes physically. You're exhausted in a way that rest can't seem to fix.

Here's what makes founder burnout so disorienting: it doesn't just make you tired- it makes you question everything.

You start wondering:
- Am I still the right person to lead this?
- Did I choose the wrong path?
- Is this just a phase - or am I done?
- Why does this feel so heavy all the time?

And underneath those questions is something even harder: the fear that stepping away or slowing down would be a betrayal.

Of your team. Of your audience. Of the past version of you who believed in this dream with everything they had.

That's the grief that rarely gets talked about - the grief of falling out of love with the thing you built. Or worse, realising it's no longer a reflection of who you are.

We have a certain image in our heads of what burnout looks like: someone crying in the shower, unable to get out of bed, missing deadlines, forgetting how to spell their own name.

But that's the extreme end. Most founder burnout looks nothing like that.

Most of the time, burnout looks like over-functioning. You're not doing less - you're doing more. You're hustling, multitasking, saying yes to everything. You're so determined not to fall behind that you forget to check if you've already run out of fuel.

The problem is, high-functioning burnout is easier to ignore. You're still productive. You're still responsive. But you're running on fumes, and eventually, the engine sputters. See this isn't just burnout. It's an emotional reckoning. And while it's deeply uncomfortable, it's also a turning point but not one that is easy to see.

Isolation deepens the problem and makes burnout worse. Because as entrepreneurs, it's baked in isn't it? We are expected to be self-starters, motivators, optimists. We are seen as people who make things happen, who solve problems, who never stop pushing forward. You might have a partner or friends, but they don't fully understand the pressure. And even in founder communities, there's often an unspoken rule to keep things positive, polished, and impressive.

Nobody wants to be the one saying, "Actually, I'm struggling."

And so, when the fog creeps in, many founders hide it. We continue performing the role of the founder while feeling increasingly disconnected from ourselves. We show up with a smile and deliver the pitch, all the while internally counting the hours until we can log off and just be quiet.

Even in communities built for entrepreneurs, there's often a reluctance to speak openly about this emotional fatigue. The culture of relentless positivity- of celebrating wins, sharing milestones, and always being "on it"- leaves little room for honesty about what it feels like when the joy is gone. Founders fear being seen as weak. They fear that revealing their exhaustion might undermine their credibility. They fear, most of all, that if they stop for a second, everything will fall apart. Part of what wears founders down isn't just the work- it's the weight. The mental spinning plates.

You hold space for clients. You coach your team. You write the marketing copy. You reassure your family. You pitch, produce, plan, deliver, and troubleshoot.

And in all that holding, you forget to hold space for yourself.

When you're the safety net for everyone else, who catches you?

So instead, we post our wins. We celebrate the milestones. We talk about the new client, the sold-out launch, the press feature, while quietly wondering if anyone else feels like they're losing their mind.

There's also a grief that comes with realising your business is taking more than it gives. For some, it arrives suddenly, perhaps when they miss a family moment they'd promised to be present for, or when they realise they haven't felt truly rested in months. For others, the awareness builds gradually: a string of half-hearted launches, a resistance to innovation, a quiet resentment toward clients or team members who ask for more than you can give.

The fog doesn't just steal energy. It steals vision. You lose the ability to imagine the future because the present feels so heavy. You stop dreaming. You stop planning. You start surviving.

It's at this point that many founders start to question everything. Is this business really what I want? Was it ever? Why does it feel so hard all the time? Why am I the only one feeling this way? What if I'm just not cut out for this?

These questions are painful, not just because they raise doubt, but because they threaten identity. When you've poured years into a business, when it's been your creative outlet, your income, your validation, your challenge - facing the possibility that it's no longer right for you feels like betrayal. Not just of the business, but of the version of yourself who believed in it so completely.

Founder Identity Collapse - When You *Are* the Business

One of the most disorienting things about running a business is how quickly *you become it*. You don't just run a startup - you *are* the startup. Every win feels like a personal validation. Every setback? A referendum on your worth.

It starts innocently enough. You say "we" when you mean "me." You check your Stripe dashboard like it's a mood ring.

You start introducing yourself not with your name, but with what you do. Before long, you're not sure where *you* end and your pitch deck begins.

And then something breaks. A launch flops. A key hire quits. You don't hit the numbers. And suddenly, it's not just the business that's struggling - it's *you*. Your confidence, your sense of purpose, even your basic self-worth can start to wobble.

This is what I call **Founder Identity Collapse**. It's the quiet unraveling that happens when your identity is entirely tethered to your business's success - and no one told you what to do when that success stalls.

Here's what it looks like in real life:

- You feel guilty for taking a day off - even if it's a funeral or your own birthday.
- Someone asks how you are, and your answer is yep doing great, followed by your revenue number.
- You can't remember what you used to talk about before you had a business.
- You dread networking because you feel like a has-been - even though nothing's *actually* failed yet.

The truth is, you are not your business. It's something you've built - not who you are. And when that line blurs, burnout, shame, and paralysis creep in.

So if you're in that place right now - feeling like your business's struggle is a personal character flaw - let me tell you something tender and true:

You are still whole, even when your company is in pieces.

Your value doesn't live in a dashboard.

And when you finally let your business just be a business - something separate, something not so sacred - you get to be a human again. A very tired, very brave, and still very capable human.

Getting out

All of this emotional reckoning is essential. And yet, so many founders try to skip over it. They try to fix the fog by changing tactics. They launch something new. They hire a coach. They rebrand. And while all of these things can help, they often serve as distractions if done prematurely. Because the truth is, no tactic will work if the problem is not strategy, but depletion.

The way out of founder fog is not a productivity hack. It is not a better calendar or a new system. It is rest and honesty. Creating a space for a deep and sometimes uncomfortable reckoning with where you are, what you feel, and what you truly want. Let's be honest about something else here: founders are terrible at resting. Rest feels unproductive. Indulgent. Guilt-inducing. Like something you have to earn.

But here's the truth: you don't get a medal for burning out.

There's no bonus round for dragging yourself to the finish line with a broken ankle and a laptop in your hand. No client is thanking you for replying to emails at 11pm. No investor is awarding extra points for insomnia and imposter syndrome.

You don't need permission to rest. You need a plan to protect it.

For some, this honesty leads to micro-adjustments- cutting back, taking real breaks, delegating more, reconnecting with the parts of the business that bring joy.

For others, the honesty leads to bigger changes- pausing the business, closing it, or shifting direction entirely.

What matters is that the honesty comes first.

Recovery, when it begins, is often subtle. It looks like walking without headphones for the first time in weeks, just to hear your own thoughts. It looks like reaching out to a peer and admitting you're tired. It looks like reading something unrelated to business, or spending a day offline without guilt. Recovery from founder fog doesn't start with a big revelation. It starts with small moments. Micro acts of rebellion against the grind.

- Saying no to a meeting that doesn't matter.
- Taking a Wednesday morning to go for a walk instead of staring at your inbox.
- Asking a peer, "Do you ever feel like this too?"
- Putting your phone down at 8pm and letting the world wait.
- Going to bed on time. On a weekday. Just because.

These aren't huge things. But they're signals. You're sending yourself the message: I matter too.

And slowly, it shifts. The fog begins to lift. The colours return. You find yourself laughing again.
You notice small moments of joy. You feel curious again. You take your foot off the gas and realise the car is still moving.

The business may or may not survive this reckoning. But the founder must.

And that's the heart of this chapter: you cannot build something sustainable if you are not sustainable.

You cannot lead with vision if your inner world is clouded. You cannot serve others if you are constantly emptying yourself. Sometimes, recovery means stepping away. For a weekend. A month. Longer. Sometimes, it means hiring help - even if it pinches financially- because your health is the real investment.

Sometimes, it means restructuring your business to serve your life, not the other way around. And sometimes, yes, it means letting go entirely.

Let me say it clearly: **choosing your wellbeing over your business is not failure**. It is what I did, and I believe it is the most radical, responsible form of leadership.

Because what good is a thriving business if it costs you your peace, your health, or your identity?

We do not talk enough about the human cost of entrepreneurship. We celebrate tenacity but rarely question the toll. We idolise resilience but gloss over recovery. We reward consistency but ignore context. And so, founders suffer quietly, convinced that struggle is just the price of ambition.

But it doesn't have to be.

There is a version of entrepreneurship that honours your health, your time, your relationships. There is a way to build that doesn't require burnout as a badge of honour. There is value in enough. There is power in saying no. There is wisdom in pausing. And there is immense strength in admitting that you are tired - and that you deserve to feel well again.

This chapter is not an instruction manual. It won't give you a five-step fix. But it is an invitation.

To check in with yourself. To look beyond the metrics and milestones. To ask not just how the business is doing - but how you are doing. You are not a machine. Your worth is not in your output. You can slow down without falling behind. You can pause without losing everything. You're allowed to change your mind. You don't owe anyone your exhaustion. You're not the only one feeling this way.

Because you matter. Your energy matters. Your joy matters.

And no vision, no business, no dream is worth sacrificing the whole of yourself for.

Let's Redefine Success

Imagine if success wasn't just revenue, reach, or recognition - but also:

- Waking up without dread
- Having a weekend without your laptop
- Feeling excited about your work again
- Having space to think, not just react
- Building a business that supports your life - not consumes it

That's the version of entrepreneurship I want for you.

Final Thought: You Matter More Than Your Metrics

This chapter isn't about fixing burnout overnight. It's about seeing it clearly- and choosing not to pretend anymore.

The fog doesn't mean you've failed. It means something's asking to be heard. And when you listen to it - truly listen - you get to choose a better way forward.

Because your energy matters. Your voice matters. And most of all, *you* matter.

Not as a founder. Not as a brand. But as a human being with a heart, a limit, and a life beyond the business.

And if nobody's told you this lately: **you're doing enough. And you are enough**.

Even in the fog.

Interlude - What we wish you knew...A Note from the Trenches: Your Strategy Isn't the Problem

Contributed by Mike Weston - Escape Velocity, who works tirelessly with founders to create headspace for founders, and to help them unravel AI for strategic advantage, not just efficiency - he is great at helping building unshakeable SMEs.

Your strategy isn't the problem. Read that again.

The fact that it's stale, that the market has shifted, that revenue has flatlined—these are not the disease. They are symptoms.

The disease is your operational model. You have become the most expensive firefighter in your own company. While you've been busy solving today's problems, you've lost the ability to build the systems that prevent tomorrow's. Your business isn't failing because your vision is wrong; it's failing because the business is running *you*, not the other way around.

The trap most founders fall into here is trying to find a *new* strategy. They'll go to an offsite, create a new slide deck, and feel a brief hit of clarity. But that new plan will be dead within weeks, suffocated by the same operational chaos that killed the last one. You cannot execute a new strategy from inside the engine room.

The work isn't to find a "perfect" plan. It's to escape the operational chaos so that a relevant strategy has room to emerge.

This is a two-step intervention. It is brutally simple.

Step 1: Triage. Reclaim 15 Minutes Daily.

Your most valuable asset is strategic headspace, and you currently have none. Before any new strategy can work, you must create space for it to breathe.

Action: Identify your three most repetitive daily tasks. Use AI to handle the first draft of these (emails, updates, client responses). This isn't revolutionary, it's surgical. Protect those reclaimed minutes as sacred strategy time.

Step 2: Diagnostic. Challenge Your Core Assumption.

In that protected time, don't "think harder", ask better questions. Use AI as an objective sparring partner.

Action: Give your AI tool real data (anonymized client feedback, service descriptions, competitor analysis) and ask: "What is the single biggest assumption our business is making that's most likely to be false in today's market?" Then sit with the discomfort of the answer.

You don't need a better strategy. You need the operational breathing room for strategy to exist. Fix the system, and clarity will follow.

Chapter 9

When the Plan Fails - Strategy Stagnation & Market Shifts

When the Strategy That Built the Business No Longer Works

Every business begins with a plan.

A dream, dressed up in a slide deck. A vision that made perfect sense in the early days - full of hope, full of hustle. You'd been on a course, an incubator, an accelerator, read a few Start Up success books. You had your value proposition nailed, your ideal customer in mind, and your plan of action (or at least a napkin sketch of one) ready to roll. You knew what made you different. You knew who you were here to help. And for a while, that was more than enough.

The work started rolling in. Clients said yes. Sales came through. Your message resonated, your gut instincts proved right more often than wrong, and the systems - scrappy as they were - mostly held. You were figuring it out as you went, of course, but the wheels were turning. Forward momentum was real.
Until...it wasn't.

Maybe growth slowed, and you couldn't quite explain why. Maybe costs crept up in the background while you were too busy doing the day to day firefighting to notice. Maybe customers shifted - what they wanted, how they bought, who they trusted - and you missed it. Or maybe it was your competitors who changed the game, while you were still playing by the old rules.

And then one day, somewhere between the third coffee and another late-night spreadsheet, it hits you. You're still doing all the things that used to work.But they're not working anymore. Welcome to strategy stagnation.

And if this sounds familiar, know this: you're far from alone. It happens more often than anyone likes to admit - even to the best, most capable, most passionate founders.

This chapter is about what to do when your business stops responding to the original plan. It's more than the customer issue in Chapter 3. It's about how to spot the signs before they quietly pile up into a full-blown crisis. It's about how to respond to changing market conditions without spiralling into panic or stuck-in-the-head inertia.

Because markets move. People evolve. Behaviour shifts. And if your business strategy doesn't adapt too, you risk quietly slipping into irrelevance - all while working harder than ever to hold things together.

The Illusion of "Working"

One of the riskiest stages in any business isn't a dramatic crisis. It's the quiet, unremarkable stretch where things are... fine. Not amazing. Not terrible. Just... fine.

Revenue is trickling in. People respond to you on LinkedIn. The bills are mostly paid. You're busy enough to feel busy, but the spark has dulled. The clarity that fuelled you in the early days is now clouded by questions you don't have the energy to answer. You're working harder than ever - longer hours, more hats, fewer boundaries - but the returns just don't match the effort.

You tell yourself it's seasonal, or even political. That things will bounce back. That it's a blip, a fluke, a weird quarter. But somewhere in the back of your mind, there's a quiet knowing: this isn't just a dip.
It's a drift.

As one founder put it to me:

"I thought it was just a quiet patch. But when I looked back over the last 12 months, I realised I'd been in a slow decline for most of them. I just didn't want to admit it. I didn't want it to be true."

And that's the thing about stagnation - it rarely arrives with flashing lights and dramatic music.
It creeps in.
It whispers.
It settles into your systems, your mindset, your team. Until you start believing that the plateau you're on is all you can hope for.

But here's the truth: strategy isn't a one-time decision. It's a living thing. And every so often, it needs reviewing, rewriting - sometimes replacing altogether.
The hard part is knowing when to hold your nerve, and when to make the leap.

The Early Warning Signs of a Strategy That's Gone Stale

So how do you know your strategy might need a rethink?
Here are the common flags:
1. Revenue Has Flatlined
If your income hasn't grown in 6–12 months (despite increased effort), it's a sign the current strategy has run out of steam.
2. Your Acquisition Costs Keep Climbing
You're spending more to get each customer - while returns shrink. Marketing is eating margin.
3. Engagement Has Dropped Off
Your audience isn't responding like they used to. Open rates dip. Social feels quiet. Offers get fewer bites.

4. You're Working Harder for Smaller Wins

Effort is up. Results are down. Everything feels harder than it should.

5. Your Offer Hasn't Changed in Years

You haven't evolved what you're selling- even though the world around you has.

6. Your Business Feels Slightly... Out of Step

It's hard to pinpoint, but something about your positioning, pricing, or delivery feels a little off. Like the market has moved on - and you forgot to follow.

Why Even Smart Strategies Stop Working

Before you beat yourself up, let's be clear: this happens to everyone. Even brilliant businesses hit this wall. Here's why:

1. The Market Shifts

What worked in 2022 might flop in 2025. Look at how AI is upending everything right now. Business systems are evolving. Consumer needs evolve. Competitors emerge. Global events change priorities overnight (remember that year?).

2. You've Outgrown Your Original Model

What made sense at year one doesn't necessarily work at year four. You're solving bigger problems now - but still using the same small tools.

3. Your Competitors Got Better

They adjusted. Innovated. Integrated new tools. Hired the help you've been putting off. And now they're picking off your customers one by one.

4. You Clung to Familiarity

It's human nature. If something "still kind of works," it feels risky to change it. But slow erosion rarely feels urgent - until it's irreversible.

5. You're Too Tired to Be Visionary

When you're running on empty, it's easier to stick with what you know. Even if it's no longer effective. Innovation feels like a luxury.

Doing a Strategy Health Check

Before you start burning it all down, spend hours getting overwhelmed by new technology options, or launching ten new offers, pause.

Do a strategic audit. Ask yourself:

- ☐ What part of the business is still growing?
- ☐ Where is performance flat - or dropping?
- ☐ Which bits of my business are repetitive where I could introduce AI to help?
- ☐ What's changed in my customer's world?
- ☐ What am I still doing out of habit, not effectiveness?
- ☐ If I had to start from scratch - what would I do differently?

The goal isn't to create more work. It's to get honest. Because clarity beats urgency every time.

The Market Doesn't Owe You Relevance

One of the hardest pills to swallow is this: just because something used to work doesn't mean it still should. Customers evolve. Priorities shift. Technology leaps ahead. And the market doesn't wait for you to catch up.

The job of your strategy is to keep your business relevant - not just operational.

Here's how to start reconnecting with reality:

1. Reconnect With Your Customers

Build on the conversations we discussed in Chapter 3.

Talk to them. Interview your audience.

This time ask questions specific to your sector, industry or the challenges you think your business solves for them:

What's frustrating you right now?

What's changed in the past year?

What would make your life easier?

They'll often tell you exactly what is happening in the real world.

2. Review Your Value Proposition

Is your messaging still speaking to their needs? Is it clear, simple, and focused on outcomes they care about? Or is it clinging to old pain points?

3. Rethink Your Pricing & Packaging

Are your offers aligned with current spending habits? Is there a simpler or more accessible version you could create?

4. Watch the Numbers - Early

Don't wait until you're in freefall. A 10% drop in any aspect of your business is a warning. A 30% dip is a strategy problem. A 50% dip is a rebuild.

Making the Decision to Pivot

A pivot doesn't mean scrapping everything. It means making intentional, strategic shifts in response to what you're seeing. It might mean:

- Changing your core audience
- Tweaking your offer and narrowing it to the most profitable element
- Introducing new off the shelf operational tools to get things organised behind the scenes
- Shifting your pricing model (recurring revenue instead of one offs)
- Reposition your business and purpose around a clearer, more urgent customer outcome

What matters is intentional change, not reactive panic.

Ask:

- What is no longer working in this business - it could be a piece of equipment, it might be a member of the team?
- What is still working - and can it be leveraged?
- What would I do differently if I started today?

"A pivot isn't failure. It's an upgrade. A smarter version of your old strategy."

Examples of Strategic Pivots

In the wake of the pandemic, **Dishoom**, the much-loved Indian restaurant chain known for its lively café culture, faced the stark reality of shuttered venues and a halted hospitality industry. But instead of going dark, they pivoted swiftly and thoughtfully. They launched "Dishoom at Home" - a DIY kit that allowed customers to recreate their iconic bacon naan rolls and house black daal from their own kitchens. The pivot wasn't just a revenue stream; it deepened brand connection during isolation and created a new national audience that wouldn't have stepped through a London location.

What began as a temporary solution has grown into a permanent and profitable product line, proving that even the most experience-based businesses can translate their magic beyond bricks and mortar.

Meanwhile, **Fever-Tree**, originally known for revolutionising the premium tonic water market, quietly diversified its focus as consumer habits shifted. As demand for at-home mixology surged, they leaned into direct-to-consumer offerings, bundling mixers with curated cocktail recipes and expanding into low- and no-alcohol pairings to reflect changing drinking culture. Instead of clinging to their core tonic range, they widened their product scope while staying true to their brand ethos: quality, sophistication, and experience. The result? Sustained growth in an uncertain market, and a stronger brand relevance beyond the bar cart.

An example of how one of my consultancy clients are pivoting to take advantage of AI in their business is rooted in moving them from bespoke consulting to a scalable AI-Powered platform.

Their revenue like many consultants was limited by time constraints and chasing new contracts. So they used AI to codify their expertise into a **self-service compliance and culture tool,** they:

- Trained an LLM on anonymised past audit reports and regulatory documents.
- Built a "Compliance Copilot" for SMEs that scans HR policies, contracts, and handbooks for gaps against current law.

- Added a founder-friendly dashboard with risk scoring and recommendations (with an upsell for human review).

Clever part:

- **Moved from project-based revenue → SaaS recurring revenue**.
- **Kept consultancy as premium tier** ("AI flags, human fixes").
- **Widened the market** - instead of just clients who could afford a £10k audit, they now have thousands of SMEs paying £99/month.
- **Positioned as a hybrid trust model** - AI for speed and scale, humans for reassurance.

Within 18 months, they 4×'d revenue, halved the founder's delivery load, and gained valuation uplift because they looked like a tech-enabled business rather than a consultancy.

Each pivot came from listening, not guessing.

Strategy Isn't a One-Time Document

Your business strategy should evolve like software. Think of your strategy like an app. You wouldn't launch version 1.0 and never update it again. You'd patch bugs, release updates, add features based on feedback. Same goes for business strategy. Make it a habit to review and refine.

Schedule:
- Quarterly reviews
- Annual deep dives
- Post-launch debriefs
- Customer research days

Don't wait for a dip. Build responsiveness into your rhythm.

If You've Waited Too Long

First: be kind to yourself. You're not the only one who's blinked and realised the plan stopped working six months ago.

Second: start anyway.

Even if your runway is shorter. Even if the market is louder. Even if the team is weary. The longer you delay, the harder it becomes. But there's always a path forward. No one has it all under control - or, in the case of AI know everything and are miles ahead of you.

So start - Even if it's messy. Even if it's slow. Even if you're scared.

Start.

Checklist: Strategy Health Check

- ☐ Revenue is growing year-on-year
- ☐ Customer acquisition and the costs relating to getting customers, is stable or improving
- ☐ Your offer aligns with what your market currently values
- ☐ You're still excited about your direction
- ☐ Competitor activity doesn't worry you
- ☐ Your model supports profit- not just effort and hustle

If three or more are missing, it's time to review.

Final Thought: The Best Founders Don't Predict. They Respond. You don't need to be a genius strategist. You don't need to understand or even use AI or technology right now. You don't need to have a five-year plan carved into stone.

What you need is responsiveness. A willingness to ask hard questions. To see clearly. To adapt before the market forces your hand.

Because the founders who build businesses that last?

They're not the ones with the flashiest launches.

They're the ones who evolve - again and again.

And again.

Interlude - What They Wish You Knew... Rewriting Resilience

Contributed by Quinton McAffie. Co-Founder of Social Places, and a leading South African Entrepreneur who has made his location based tech marketing agency a success.

One of the hardest truths I've had to learn is that strategy isn't something you can build - or sustain - alone. You can draft the plans, set the targets, even will them into life for a while. But over time, if the strategy isn't being lived and tested by a team, it stalls.

When we started Social Places, my co-founder and I thought sheer drive would be enough. We worked late nights, launched scrappy MVPs, tried to bootstrap our way forward. What I wish I'd known back then is that strategy can't be a solo act. Holding on too tightly - whether to equity, decisions, or "the plan" itself - narrows your view just when you need it most.

The biggest turning point for us came when we brought others into the journey, not just as employees but as shareholders, leaders, and partners. I thought giving up control meant losing something. I realise now what it really meant was gaining the strengths, perspectives, and resilience I didn't have on my own.

You see it in how our team talks about their work.

Kayla, who runs operations, once said to me: *"Resilience in ops isn't flashy - it's steady. It's building systems that hold under pressure so others can thrive."* That line stuck with me. Strategy doesn't survive without that kind of foundation.

Orestes, our CTO, puts it differently: *"Most real problems are like a tangled web, not a straight line between two dots."*

He's right. As founders, we love clean plans, straight lines, elegant decks. But reality is messier, and you need people around you who actually thrive in that complexity.

Our head of finance, Rose, taught me another lesson. We once invested heavily in a software solution that turned out to be fundamentally wrong for our model. It would've been easy to keep throwing money at it - but she pushed us to cut our losses. Her take? *"Resilient organisations are the ones willing to stop funding yesterday and pivot to tomorrow."* That saved us from sinking deeper.

And then there's Tracey in HR, who reminds me constantly that strategy without people is just theory. As she puts it: *"Your product is nothing without the people who build it, sell it, and believe in it. If they're not motivated, you have no strategy at all."*

Looking back, the real growth of Social Places didn't come from the original plan. It came from the points where that plan failed, and the team helped me reimagine it. The lesson I wish I'd absorbed sooner is this: don't treat strategy as a document you own. Treat it as a living thing that only survives if others breathe life into it.

So if you're stuck, facing stagnation or a market shift, ask yourself: who else needs to be in the room? Who can see the blind spots you're missing? And what are you willing to let go of so that the strategy can move again?

That's where the real breakthroughs happen.

Chapter 10

Behind on Everything: Debt, Deadlines & Decision Time

When Borrowed Time Becomes Borrowed Money

There's a moment - maybe it's when your bank card declines unexpectedly, or when another red envelope hits the doormat - where you realise you're not just behind on a few bills.

You're behind on everything.

Emails. Invoices. VAT returns. Rent. Sleep. And that creeping sense of dread you've been trying to ignore? It's now moved in permanently and rearranged the furniture.

Debt is one of the most common - and yet least openly discussed - parts of running a business. And as I have mentioned before the Blue Chip Corporates don't exactly set a good example.

It often starts with good intentions. You take out a small loan to invest in growth. Use a credit card to cover a slow month. Maybe delay one payment to make another. It's not reckless. It's practical.

Until it isn't.

Because when revenue dips, costs rise, or cash flow hits a bottleneck, those manageable chunks of borrowing can quickly pile up into something monstrous. And what started as a clever cash bridge starts to look and feel like a trap.

Creditors start calling. Payments get delayed. Overdrafts hit their limit. And the mental toll? It's immense.

In this chapter, we'll look at the real impact of business debt - financially, legally, emotionally - and how UK-based business owners can navigate creditors, restructure responsibly, survive the stress of owing more than you can pay back, and how to protect your sanity and reputation through it.

Business debt doesn't always look like disaster at first. Sometimes, it's just what you need to get things moving. A startup loan. A Bounce Back Loan. A bit of credit to cover a bulk order or invest in a new system.

It can be smart. Strategic. Necessary.

But when the sales don't land, or the client ghosted you after the deposit, or the quiet season is *a bit quieter than usual*, debt becomes something else entirely. It becomes a weight. A slow-burn panic. An invisible but ever-present tension in your chest every time you look at your bank balance. Let's be clear: getting into debt doesn't mean you've failed. It means you've tried to keep things going. And you're not alone. Debt doesn't mean you made bad decisions. It often means you were trying to make good ones - with the information and tools you had at the time.

Why Debt Happens (Even to Smart Founders)

Here are the most common reasons founders find themselves juggling debt:

1. Growth Ambition

You borrowed to scale. New staff, new website, bigger space. The numbers made sense on paper- until they didn't. But when reality didn't match the forecast, the repayments kept coming.

2. Unexpected Shortfalls

Sales dipped. A client pulled out then ghosted you. That deal you were relying on fell through.

Suddenly, the short-term loan became a crutch and now it's a high interest long-term problem.

3. Seasonal Gaps

You knew there'd be slow months. You used credit cards or overdrafts to tide you over. You planned to catch up next quarter. Then next quarter didn't go to plan.

4. Pandemic Fallout or Economic Shocks

Let's not forget: the past few years were brutal. For many, Bounce Back Loans or tax deferrals were lifelines. But now they're due- and they're heavier than they looked.

> **"I never meant to take on debt. I just kept borrowing a little here and there to keep things moving. Then one day, the repayments were bigger than the income."**
> **- UK-based service founder**

What Debt *Feels* Like

Debt is not just a number in a spreadsheet. It's a pressure that lives in your nervous system.

It looks like:

- Avoiding bank notifications like they're cursed scrolls
- Your heart racing every time the phone rings
- Making deals with yourself about "which bill can wait"
- Going to bed with your mind racing at 2am, calculating who to pay first tomorrow
- Dreading tax season more than root canal
- Feeling ashamed to tell your partner, your staff, or your parents

Debt messes with your decision-making. It clouds your clarity, feeds your self-doubt, and makes you feel like you're always one missed payment away from losing everything.

And worst of all? It isolates you. Because debt comes with shame. And shame makes you go quiet.

But here's the truth: silence only makes it worse.

The Many Flavours of Business Debt

Let's decode the different types, so you know what you're dealing with.

1. Business Loans

These might be traditional bank loans, startup loans, or even that £5k you borrowed from your brother. Some are secured (against assets), some unsecured but come loaded with emotional and personal implications. They usually have set terms and fixed repayments, and it's worse if they don't.

2. Credit Cards or Overdrafts

Flexible, yes - but also expensive if you're carrying balances long-term. Easy to access, hard to pay down.

3. Bounce Back Loans (BBLs)

Cheap interest, fast approval - but many founders are now facing repayments they didn't plan for. The UK offered many schemes like this to help businesses after the 2020/21 pandemic, and still offer many more debt based schemes to support small businesses survive today and will undoubtedly continue to in the future. Small business makes up a big part of the UK economy and I'm not sure that things aren't going to get harder over the coming years. A helping hand from the government is great, especially when we all know how little help a founder can get from anywhere else. But the reality is that if you don't plan for those repayments then they will still come and bite you on the bum.

4. HMRC Arrears

VAT, PAYE, and Corporation Tax. They're easy to delay... and stressful to catch up on. And HMRC has teeth. Sharp ones.

5. Supplier Debt

This includes unpaid invoices to freelancers, suppliers, wholesalers, landlords, manufacturers, or agencies. Delaying them might buy time - but it damages trust. And practically anyone can call in a debt and draw unwanted attention to a financially precarious business.

If it is all going to pot and you are scared about the implications of your debt, don't be. It is never, ever insurmountable. Never. And there are many organisations out there who can help whether your debt is business or personal. Get help immediately and remember with the right advice it can be possible to release the debt and live your life again afterwards with much more peace than you had before.

Let's look at the facts.

The UK Legal Landscape Around Debt

In the UK, business debt is treated differently depending on your **business structure**:

- **Sole Traders** are personally liable for all debts

- **Limited Companies** are separate legal entities (unless you've signed personal guarantees - please don't if you can avoid it)

If you're unsure, check:

- Loan documents for the fine print on personal guarantees
- Lease agreements for liability clauses - do they name you or the company?
- Whether credit has been extended to you or the company
- What the informal email was agreeing terms with your brother

Knowing your liability is the first step to knowing what to do next.

What Creditors Actually Do (And How It Escalates)

Creditors don't usually leap straight to court. There's a process.

- **Early Stage:** Polite reminders. A couple of emails. Maybe a phone call offering to discuss terms.
- **Middle Stage:** More aggressive emails. Interest starts adding up. They might pass you to a collection agency.
- **Late Stage:** Legal notices. County Court Judgements (CCJs). In the case of companies- winding-up petitions.

"Once the letters from debt collectors started arriving, I felt physically sick. It was all I could think about. I couldn't even focus on client work."
- Retail founder, Manchester

It doesn't always get that far. But if you ignore the early stages, you give creditors no choice but to push harder.

What to Do When You Can't Pay

First things first: *don't panic.* Panic leads to avoidance. Avoidance makes things worse.

1. Face the Numbers

Make a complete list. Who do you owe, how much, and what are the terms? Include due dates, interest rates, and any arrears. Yes, it's terrifying. But it's also empowering. Clarity is your first tool.

2. Prioritise

HMRC and your team come first - they have legal weight. Next, deal with secured loans (miss a payment here, and assets can be repossessed). Then work your way through unsecured debts.

3. Communicate Early

The sooner you contact creditors, the more likely they'll be flexible. Explain. Be honest. Propose a plan. Ask for a pause. Most would rather recoup something than chase you through court.

4. Get Expert Help

This is not the time to wing it.

Speak to:

- **Business Debtline** – free, confidential advice
- **Your accountant** – they may spot options you've missed
- **An insolvency practitioner** – especially for limited companies facing serious trouble, it was three free conversations with an insolvency practitioner over two

years, (every time I got nervous) that gave me a lot of useful advice and definitely helped me work out what to do to move forwards.

5. Consider Formal Options

There are systems in place for when you *can't* repay everything:

- **Time to Pay Arrangements (HMRC)** – gives you more time
- **Debt Management Plan (DMP)** – usually for sole traders
- **Company Voluntary Arrangement (CVA)** – restructure company debt while continuing to trade
- **Individual Voluntary Arrangement (IVA)** – for personal debt tied to your business
- **Administration or liquidation** – if closing down becomes the safest choice

I cover the last three of these in more detail in Chapter 11.

If You're Being Chased...

- **Stay calm.** You are not the first or last person to owe money.
- **Ask for everything in writing.** No decisions over the phone.
- **Don't admit liability without advice.** You could lock yourself into unnecessary commitments.
- **Keep a paper trail.** Every call, email, or text. Document everything.
- **Don't ignore legal letters.** If you receive a court document, respond promptly. Ignoring it can lead to a default judgement against you.

You have more rights and options than you might think.

Protecting Your Mental Health in the Middle of Money Stress

Money trouble doesn't just hit your bank- it hits your body, your sleep, your relationships, and your confidence. Debt stress is real. And relentless.

Here's how to survive it:

- **Set time boundaries.** Don't spend all day checking balances or rewriting the same list of debts.
- **Create a "circle of sanity."** One or two trusted people you can talk to. No pretending. No shame.
- **Seek professional mental health support.** Therapy, coaching, or peer groups can make a huge difference.
- **Take breaks.** Go for a walk. Watch something silly. Dance in your kitchen. Even ten minutes off matters.
- **Avoid unhealthy coping.** Overworking, drinking, doomscrolling- they don't help. Be gentle with yourself.

You are not your debt. You are not a failure. You're a human doing your best in a tough situation.

How to Prioritise When Everything's on Fire

When the to-do list is longer than your runway, and everything feels urgent, it's time to step back and sort the mess. This isn't about perfection. It's about doing the next right thing.

1. Stop. Breathe. Triage.

Before rushing into action, pause. Triage isn't about doing everything - it's about identifying what's bleeding.

- What's urgent *and* irreversible if not dealt with?
- What can safely wait 48 hours?

- What feels urgent but isn't actually critical?

2. Stabilise the business, not the inbox.
Answering emails isn't prioritising - it's reacting. Ask:

- What's the one thing that keeps the lights on this week?
- Is there a customer, supplier or staff member who needs clarity to keep moving?

3. Find your cashflow cliff.
Forget vanity metrics. What's your actual financial runway?

- How many weeks of cash do you have left?
- What income is realistic in that time?
- What's draining your cash the fastest?

4. Protect core relationships.
If you disappear or spiral, people start guessing. That's when trust breaks.

- Who needs to hear from you this week to prevent escalation?
- Be honest without panicking. Clarity buys you grace.

5. Choose one win to chase.
Even in the mess, you need momentum.

- What's one thing you can actually complete today or this week?
- A paid invoice, a final proposal sent, a conversation that unblocks something - anything that shifts the energy forward.

6. Postpone, Pause or Let Go.
Not everything can be saved - and not everything should.

- Are you holding onto a "should" that's draining resources (e.g. a half-built feature, an event, a client who's gone cold)?
- What can be paused or parked to free up headspace?

7. Ask for help before it's too late.

Silence isn't strength. It's stress with a mute button.

- Who can give you 30 mins of perspective?
- Where could you swap pride for progress?

Get to a point where you can handle this checklist and tick everything on it;

- ☐ I know exactly how much I owe and to whom
- ☐ I've prioritised urgent creditors
- ☐ I've contacted creditors where needed
- ☐ I have a repayment or restructure plan
- ☐ I've sought advice, not just guessed
- ☐ I'm tracking the emotional toll and seeking support

Moving Forward: From Debt to Recovery

Debt doesn't have to be the end. Many very successful businesses have had debt- lots of it. Some still do. What separates those that recover from their debt being out of control and those that don't is *action*.

Not just hustle. Not panic. Not hiding behind a new product launch to mask the fear.

Clear, honest action.

Start where you are. Get advice. Ask for help. Make a plan. Stick to it.

You might repay every penny. You might renegotiate. You might walk away and rebuild something stronger. All of those paths are valid.

> **"I thought the debt meant I'd failed. But in facing it, I became a better founder. More disciplined. More aware. More human."**

You haven't failed. You're in a rough patch. But you're not alone - and you're not done.

There is life after debt.

There is clarity after the chaos.

There is recovery after the storm.

And it begins now.

Interlude - What They Wish You Knew...

Debt is Noisy

Advice from Chris Worden, founder of Director First, and someone you can count on for clear, compassionate guidance on debt and recovery for UK directors and founders.

Debt is noisy. It gets into your head and tries to convince you that you are the problem. It tells you you're a bad business person, a bad parent, a bad partner. It takes ordinary business challenges and reframes them as a personal failure. If that's where you are right now, hear this: debt is a temporary financial state, not a verdict on who you are.

I've sat with hundreds of directors at the point where the letters, calls, and sleepless nights feel bigger than they are. There's a pattern I see again and again. People wait. They try to white-knuckle their way through it. They stop opening mail. They cancel meetings. They go quiet at home. And then, when they finally say it out loud - "I'm in trouble" - something shifts. Not because the numbers magically change, but because isolation does. The moment you stop carrying it alone, options appear.

Another pattern: the story you're telling yourself is harsher than the facts. You're imagining bailiffs tomorrow, bankruptcy next week, reputation in tatters. Reality is usually more procedural and slower. Creditors want clarity more than they want drama. Practically, this means you have room to breathe, make a plan, and make good decisions. Emotionally, it means you can separate your identity from your balance sheet.

A director I'll call "Aisha" came to me convinced she'd lose everything. HMRC arrears, supplier pressure, staff she cared about. She'd waited months because shame said, "You're meant to fix this alone." Once we mapped the numbers and the timeline, the picture changed.

We prioritised, communicated with suppliers and creditors, protected her personally, and closed the company the right way. Months later she messaged: "I sleep. I'm present with my kids. I'm building again." Same person. Different story. The turning point wasn't a trick, it was facing the truth with help.

Here's what I wish every founder knew in the thick of it:

- Debt is data. It's telling you something about pricing, margins, pipeline, or timing, it's not about your worth. Treat it as information not an identity.

- Silence is a tax. The longer you wait the more the options and choices fall off the table. Speak sooner, even a rough plan beats no plan.

- You can protect yourself. UK law gives Directors routes to close a company in an orderly manner and start again. The key is timing and transparency.

- You really are not your last set of accounts. Your skills, reputation with the people who matter. Your ability to create value, non of that disappears because a business model failed.

- Recovery isn't linear. There will be wobbles.

That's completely normal. Keep going. Closing a company - when it's the right move - is not the end of your story. It's an adult decision in a tough season.

When the noise is loud, borrow my belief until you can find your own: you are not finished. There is a way through. Ask for help, act early, and give yourself permission to turn the page.

Chapter 11

Closing Time - The Process of Winding Up a UK Business

Ending Doesn't Mean Failing

Let's say this early and clearly: deciding to close a business is not the same as failing. For many founders, the idea of closing a business feels like failure. It's the moment they've dreaded. The nightmare they tried to avoid at all costs.

It's not a headline you'll see in most glossy entrepreneur stories. It's rarely something shouted about on LinkedIn. But the truth is, ending something you built isn't weak. It isn't shameful. And it definitely isn't giving up. It's a decision. Often a brave one. Sometimes a smart one. And always one that deserves more credit than it gets. Sometimes, **closure is the right decision**.

You may be closing because of sustained losses. Or maybe burnout caught up with you and you've realised no business is worth sacrificing your health. Perhaps life threw you a curveball, or the market shifted under your feet. Or maybe - just maybe - the business simply served its purpose and you're ready for a new chapter - it's a valid, strategic, and very often a hugely brave move.

I write this chapter with feeling because I have literally closed businesses for all the above reasons. Whatever your reason, this chapter is your guide to navigating closure with clarity, care, and confidence. Because yes, there is a right way to end things.

And no, you don't need to go out in flames to make it meaningful.

"Closing was the best thing I ever did. It felt like failure - until I realised it was freedom."

Why Businesses Close (And Why That's Okay)

There's a misconception that closure only happens when everything's gone terribly wrong. But actually, businesses close for a whole range of reasons - and not all of them are dramatic.

Some of the most common:

- The business is no longer financially viable
- You've had a health scare or personal life change that needs your attention
- You've outgrown the business (and secretly resent it)
- A co-founder relationship soured
- The market changed and you no longer want to chase it
- You're preparing to pivot or start something new

Whatever your reason, know this: closure is part of the business lifecycle. Just like launching, scaling, or rebranding. It doesn't erase the impact you made.

Sometimes, closing the doors isn't the only way forward. Even when things are looking bleak, there are other paths that might help a business survive - or at least allow it to wind down in a way that protects what matters most. Jobs. Reputation. A clean exit. A shot at starting again. The right next step often depends on what you're trying to save. Is it the business itself? The people in it? The product, the brand, your own sanity?

The good news is: there are options. And while none of them come with a magic wand or a get-out-of-debt-free card, they do offer structured ways to either regroup, rebuild, or responsibly shut things down. Let's start with the basics:

Voluntary vs. Involuntary Closure

Let's break this down.

Voluntary Closure

- You choose to close
- It's typically done in a planned, proactive way
- Most often used for *solvent* businesses (i.e., you can pay your debts).

Involuntary Closure

- Triggered by creditors, the court, or sheer financial meltdown.
- Usually involves *insolvency*.
- Heavier on legal complexity, emotional fallout, and urgency.

This chapter will mostly focus on **voluntary** closure - because that's where you have the most control and is where I hope this book has caught you - but we'll touch on key insolvency points too.

Here's a look at some of the most common routes - beyond the immediate leap to liquidation.

Closure Routes in the UK: The Basics

Sole Traders

It's worth pausing here to say - not all of these options apply to every type of business. If you're running a limited company, you have access to formal processes like administration, CVAs, and pre-packs because your business is a separate legal entity. But if you're a sole trader, it's a different story.

Legally, you are the business, which means your personal and business finances are intertwined.

There's no "separate pot" to ring-fence. So instead of company-level procedures, sole traders usually deal with debt and closure through personal options like negotiating directly with creditors, setting up a Debt Management Plan, applying for an Individual Voluntary Arrangement (IVA), or - in the most serious cases - declaring bankruptcy.

It's still possible to wind things down responsibly or even start again, but the tools in the toolkit look different, and the stakes often feel a little more personal.

You *are* the business. There's no legal separation, so the closure is simpler (but the debts are personal).

Sole traders have fewer (and very different) options

Because sole traders *are* the business - legally and financially - there's no separation between personal and business assets. That means if the business runs into trouble, the individual's personal assets (home, savings, etc.) may also be at risk.

So, for sole traders, the options look more like:

- **Negotiating informally with creditors** (payment plans, settlements)
- **Debt Management Plans (DMPs)** or **Individual Voluntary Arrangements (IVAs)** (for personal debt restructuring)
- **Bankruptcy** (if debt is unmanageable)
- **Closing the business** and either:
    - Paying off debts over time (if possible)
    - Entering into personal insolvency processes (like IVA or bankruptcy)

You *can* still:

- Refinance or seek investment
- Sell assets or parts of the business
- Find a merger partner (though rare and informal)
- Restart under a new name (with caution and legal advice)

From a logistics perspective, here's what you need to do:

- Notify HMRC you're ceasing trading.
- File your final tax return.
- Settle any tax owed.
- Deregister from VAT or PAYE if applicable.
- Inform clients and wrap up projects.
- Keep all your records for five years.

That's it in official terms - but emotionally? That might take a little longer.

Limited Companies

Ah, the paperwork playground. As a separate legal entity, a limited company needs a more formal goodbye.

You must:

- Decide which closure route is right (more on that next).
- Notify Companies House.
- File final accounts and corporation tax returns.
- Pay off debts or appoint an insolvency practitioner (if insolvent).

Limited Company Closure Options

Sometimes, closing the doors isn't the only way forward. Even when things are looking bleak, there are other paths that might help a business survive - or at least allow it to wind down in a way that protects what matters most. Jobs. Reputation. A clean exit. A shot at starting again. The right next step often depends on what you're trying to save. Is it the business itself? The people in it? The product, the brand, your own sanity?

The good news is: there are options. And while none of them come with a magic wand or a get-out-of-debt-free card, they do offer structured ways to either regroup, rebuild, or responsibly shut things down.

Here's a look at some of the most common routes - beyond the immediate leap to liquidation.

Company Voluntary Arrangement (CVA)

Think of this as the "we just need a bit more time" route. A CVA is a formal agreement between a company and its creditors to repay what's owed over a set period - usually three to five years. It's legally binding, which gives everyone some security, and crucially, the directors stay in the driver's seat. If the business still has solid bones but is temporarily cash-strapped, a CVA can provide the breathing room it needs.

But it does rely on trust and approval - 75% of creditors (by value) need to agree to it. And you'll still need enough cash flow to stick to the repayment plan, so it's not a free pass. More like a truce, with terms.

Administration (Non-Pre-Pack)

This is a more formal move where an external administrator steps in to either rescue the business, sell it, or at the very least, make sure creditors get a better deal than they would through liquidation. It's a protective space - a kind of legal pause button - that stops creditors from taking immediate action while options are explored.

It can be useful if there's something left to salvage. But be warned: it usually means the directors hand over control, and the public nature of administration can dent the business's reputation. Not to mention, it's not cheap.

Informal Restructuring / Turnaround

If you catch the issues early enough - and if your creditors aren't already sharpening their knives - an informal turnaround might be possible. This means having frank conversations with those you owe money to, renegotiating terms, cutting costs, and getting things back on track without stepping into the formal insolvency process.

It keeps things discreet and the business in your hands, but there's no legal shield - if a creditor loses patience, they can still take action. So this route works best when relationships are strong and everyone's willing to play ball.

Scheme of Arrangement

This one's a bit of a heavyweight tool - usually reserved for larger, more complex businesses with multiple classes of creditors or shareholders. It's a court-sanctioned deal to restructure debt or ownership. Think of it as a bespoke legal contract to get everyone (or at least most people) on board with a new plan.

It's flexible and can be very effective, but it comes with a hefty dose of legal costs and complexity. So unless you're a big business with deep pockets and a legal team on speed dial, it may not be the go-to.

Debt Refinancing or Equity Injection

Sometimes, it's not about restructuring the business - it's about restructuring the money behind it. Raising new capital, either through loans or fresh investment, can give a business the boost it needs to get out of a tight spot.

Of course, this only works if investors or lenders still believe there's something worth backing.

And new funding often comes with strings attached - higher interest, reduced control, or giving up a slice of the pie. Still, if the business is fundamentally solid, this route can buy valuable time.

Asset Sales

When cash is tight, selling off non-essential or underperforming assets can free up funds and ease the pressure. It might mean parting with property, equipment, or side ventures that no longer serve the core business.

It's not a long-term fix, but it can create a short-term lifeline. Just be careful not to chop off something vital in the process - you don't want to sell the engine when the car still has somewhere to go.

Mergers or Strategic Acquisitions

Sometimes survival comes in the form of a handshake. If another company sees value in your product, people, or market share, a merger or acquisition can keep the heart of your business alive - even if it means giving up some independence.

Handled well, it can protect jobs and give the business a fresh start under new leadership. But it can also lead to tricky compromises. Culture clashes. Power struggles. And deals that, in hindsight, maybe weren't quite as strategic as they sounded in the boardroom.

Creditors' Voluntary Liquidation (CVL) - with a Restart

There are times when the business just can't be saved - but the people behind it still have the drive to start again. A CVL allows directors to voluntarily shut the company down, settle as much debt as possible, and potentially launch something new down the line.

This kind of "clean break and reboot" can be powerful - but it needs to be handled with care. If the new venture looks too much like the old one, too soon, it can raise red flags (and legal consequences) around so-called "phoenixing." So if this is the plan, get good advice and do it by the book.

Pre-Pack Administration

Now as you know from my personal experience, this one deserves its own spotlight. A pre-pack is a very specific type of administration where the business sale is arranged *before* the company officially enters administration, and it's executed the moment the administrator is appointed.

It's a bit like having your bags packed and the taxi waiting outside - fast, discreet, and often designed to preserve the value of the business without a long, public process. The buyer is frequently someone connected to the original business - even the existing directors - which can make things smoother... or spark suspicion.

Critics argue it's not always fair to creditors who are left out of the loop until after the sale's done. Supporters say it saves jobs, reduces disruption, and protects what's worth saving. Like many things in business, it depends how it's handled. A clever rescue or a backdoor deal? It all comes down to transparency and intention.

In the end, no one goes into business, planning for any of these. But knowing they exist - and understanding when each one might be the right fit - can make all the difference when you're staring down the barrel of tough decisions. Closing time doesn't always have to mean the end. Sometimes, it's just a change in direction, done with clarity and care.

Here's your checklists for the main options:

1. Voluntary Strike-Off (a.k.a. Dissolution)

Best for solvent companies that are no longer trading. This is the "I'm done, thanks for everything" route.

You must:

- Clear all debts and liabilities first.
- Distribute remaining assets (don't forget tax!).
- File a DS01 form with Companies House.
- Notify HMRC and stakeholders (legally, you must tell any interested parties).

This option works well for simple, low-asset companies. If things are clean and quiet, this is a tidy exit.

2. Members' Voluntary Liquidation (MVL)

If your company has significant assets and you want a more tax-efficient way to close, MVL could be your friend.

It involves:

- Appointing a licensed liquidator.
- Settling all liabilities.
- Distributing surplus assets to shareholders.

It's more expensive than strike-off but can save a lot in tax, especially if entrepreneurs' relief applies.

3. Creditors' Voluntary Liquidation (CVL)

This is for when things aren't going so well- i.e., you can't pay your debts. But you're still choosing to act.

It requires:

- A licensed insolvency practitioner.
- Selling company assets to repay creditors.
- A formal liquidation process.

Important: Directors can be investigated but aren't automatically penalised. Taking action early helps show you acted responsibly.

If You're Insolvent

This is the heavy bit. But it's also where good decisions matter most.

You are **insolvent** if:

- You can't pay your bills as they fall due, *or*
- Your liabilities outweigh your assets and you know you are unlikely to recover. That the money coming in, and likely to come in in the future, won't cover the debts you have now.

If this is you:

1. **Stop trading immediately.** Don't continue selling or buying.
2. **Do NOT pay off individual suppliers.** You can't give preference to one creditor over another.
3. **Contact an insolvency practitioner ASAP.**
4. **Avoid taking on new credit.** However tempting this might be, trust me it won't help.
5. **Keep all records safe and intact.**

This is no time for guesswork.

Get help, act fast, and protect yourself from personal liability (especially wrongful trading i.e. trading when you know you are insolvent and have no way of recovery in sight).

Communicating With Stakeholders

Clients

- Finish outstanding work (if you can)
- Offer referrals or refunds (if possible)
- Send a thoughtful message- people appreciate honesty and closure.

Team

- Comply with redundancy law which would be a whole chapter in itself, so research this properly - if you can't pay the money that your staff should receive by lowing their job through compulsory redundancy due to their job not existing any more, then the situation might mean they are eligible for their unpaid wages, holiday pay and redundancy owed (depending on how long they have worked for you) and will be paid via the UK Redundancy Service. This includes you too if you were on payroll and might just be a lifeline
- Provide references, recommend your team to others in your community and network
- Be honest and kind, transparent and compassionate- they're affected too

Your team is part of your legacy- treat them with care. Even if they don't do the same!

Suppliers

- Give reasonable notice
- Be honest about what you can (and can't) pay.
- Settle balances where possible (but without giving preference to one supplier over another)
- Don't ghost anyone. Professionalism here preserves your reputation- your reputation matters, it's part of your legacy too.

Final Filings & Loose Ends

If you're working with an insolvency practitioner, (and please try to, even though it costs to hire one) they'll manage most of this.

But if not, you're on the hook for the admin. Be aware that this can take up to a year to reach a final resolution and for everything to be completed in the process of closure, especially when the business is insolvent. Expect to:

- Submit a final VAT return (if registered).
- Close PAYE schemes via your payroll system.
- File final corporation tax return.
- Close business bank accounts.
- Deregister from anything HMRC-related.
- Store your records safely (you'll need to keep them for at least 6 years).

Note: If your business is insolvent, this process can take 6–12 months. Yes, it's slow. But tying it up properly gives you peace of mind.

What Happens to Debts?

If your company is solvent:

- Clear all outstanding debts before distributing assets.
- Request zero-balance confirmations.
- Inform HMRC and Companies House.

If insolvent:

- The liquidator decides who gets paid (in order of legal priority).
- Directors must not make random repayments (no "favourite" suppliers).
- Personal guarantees may be enforced (check contracts)
- Remember if you are insolvent and the assets of the business are being sold, whether through a prepack or not, you are selling the assets of the business, not the actual business itself so things like the business name have specific rules to consider
- During company administration, the desirable assets of the business are sold to the purchasing party. These assets could include stock, property, goodwill and work in progress. Prior to the sale all assets must be independently valued, which normally happens via a specialist lawyer (that you need to find the money to pay!) and the buyer must pay a fair market price.

Sole traders are personally liable - so you may need a **Debt Management Plan** or **IVA.** **This also might be worth considering if you are a Director and have liability for personal guarantees.**

What About Your Brand & Online Presence?

- Take down your website or add a closure message unless this has been included in the sale of the business as an asset
- Post a kind, clear message on your social channels.
- Deactivate social accounts or explain the exit
- Let your email list know - thank them for the journey.
- Unregister domains (or park them if you might reuse them).
- Archive testimonials, case studies, or work you may reuse

Leave a digital trail that respects your work. Give people a respectful end to the story - and make room for whatever's next.

How Long Does It All Take?

Let's be realistic:

- **Strike-Off**: around 3 months (if everything is straightforward).
- **MVL or CVL**: 6–12 months (depending on complexity and asset sales).
- **Sole trader closure**: depends mostly on your final tax deadlines.

Either way, give yourself space for admin, emotional recovery, and quiet reflection. Even unpaid closure work has value- it brings resolution. And a bit of peace in its monotony.

Plan for 3–6 months of admin, communication, and wrap-up. It can seem like a lot of unpaid time but it does leave you with a sense of completion once it is done.

Remember if you were on payroll you too can probably claim redundancy, and get unpaid Employer pension scheme payments covered so there is a small upside here.

How to End Well

OK really I think these are probably the life lessons I've absorbed from my mum, but they apply very closely to the guidelines I believe are worth following when closing your business.

- Leave no mess for others to clean up
- End things with integrity, not avoidance
- Acknowledge the value you got out of this, what worked and what didn't
- Reflect and learn your lessons
- Thank the people who supported you
- Celebrate the courage it takes to stop

"A graceful exit is a sign of maturity. Not everyone needs to build forever."

Checklist: Closing Your UK Business

- ☐ Decided on closure route
- ☐ Informed HMRC and/or Companies House
- ☐ Final accounts submitted
- ☐ Debts managed or transferred
- ☐ Stakeholders informed
- ☐ Team legally and respectfully handled
- ☐ Digital presence updated
- ☐ Records stored appropriately

Even if you can't tick them all just yet, you've started. And that's the part that counts.

Final Thoughts: The End Is Also a Beginning

You started a business. You gave it your time, your talent, your energy. That's not erased because it didn't last forever. Closure doesn't mean you failed. It means you were brave enough to *try*. Brave enough to *learn*. And wise enough to know when to let go.

You will take every hard-earned skill, every insight, and every connection into whatever comes next. Because endings - when done well- make room for new beginnings. And that? That's something to be proud of.

Interlude - What They Wish You Knew... When Walking Away Becomes the Only Option

This one is mine - a specific piece about the end, how it felt and what I have done since.

The end of Bubbl didn't come with one dramatic crash - it came with a slow, grinding realisation that we weren't going to make it.

After the failed launch, we staggered on for a while, patching holes and trying to keep investors hopeful. But deep down, my gut knew the truth: the product wasn't viable, the team wasn't aligned, and no amount of promises would turn things around.

Eventually, the only option left was a pre-pack suggested by only the investor I didn't like and who I didn't want to align with in future. On paper, it looked like a way to salvage something - protect the brand, maybe keep some of the work alive and finally get it built and out into the market with the existing tech team.

In practice, it was brutal.

Pre-packs are rarely neat, and ours was no exception. Agreements unravelled, relationships fractured, and I found myself increasingly sidelined.

Instead of orchestrating a rescue, I had to draw the line at thinly veiled WhatsApp threats about my family if I didn't fall into line, driving me to the police to get an injunction warning delivered to the investor, and leaving me feeling forced into the painful position of simply walking away.

That decision broke me. I'd poured everything into Bubbl - money, reputation, identity. It was the hub of my relationships, purpose and only source of income.

To hand it over, knowing it wasn't going to survive in any form I recognised, felt like a kind of bereavement where I'd accidentally killed the other party.

People talk about grief in personal terms, but founders know there's a version that comes with losing a business.

You mourn the future you thought you were building. You mourn the team that didn't get there and the work family that you have lost. You mourn the version of yourself who believed it would all work out.

Afterwards, I did the only thing I could: I stepped back.

I moved out of London. I took a couple of solid, successful corporate roles where nobody cared about Bubbl, and nobody asked me to pitch the impossible. It was healing, in a way. Space to rebuild my confidence, space to process. For a while, I thought that was it - my shot at building something of my own was over.

But here's the twist I didn't expect: when I reappeared in the startup scene, (because I was a little bit curious about London Tech Week and AI), I met people who knew me of old...who asked would I come and speak at an event, talk on a podcast, present a webinar, help build a community...surprise surprise all people remembered was the good.

The awards still counted. The recognition we'd earned in anticipation of Bubbl didn't vanish just because the product had. My reputation - battered in my own mind - was intact in everyone else's.

I'd been carrying shame I didn't need to carry.

That was the moment I realised: Bubbl wasn't my final story. It was my teaching story. It gave me lessons I could never have learned in any other way. And once the grief passed, those lessons became the foundation for everything I've done since.

You can find that at www.finitie.co.uk…where my aim is to make sure founders do not find themselves alone on their journey.

Chapter 12

The Emotional Fallout - Grieving, Healing & Finding Your Feet Again

What Happens After the End?

The day after a business closes is not what people imagine. There's no dramatic fade to black, no neat ending, and often, no great sense of closure at all. Instead, what many founders report is a kind of disorienting silence and the abruptness of nothing. I felt lost, and like I had no strength to focus on anything but the mundane. The adrenaline that kept everything moving- the pitch decks, the launches, the payroll panic, the endless to-do lists - is gone. In its place is a really big void.

And in that space, something unexpected begins to take hold: grief.

Entrepreneurial grief isn't always recognised. In the world of business, especially small business, the narrative tends to skip ahead. We glamorise the pivot. We celebrate the comeback. We admire the lessons learned. But very little attention is paid to the emotional wreckage in between - the hollow days, the questioning of self-worth, the quiet, persistent ache that comes from watching something you built slowly disappear.

This chapter isn't about performance. It's not about resilience or reinvention - at least, not yet. It's about what happens to you, the founder, after the emails stop, the business name gets deregistered, and the Instagram bio gets edited. It's about navigating the emotional aftermath of closing your business - and finding yourself again on the other side.

The Unseen Impact of Closure

When we talk about closing a business, the focus is often on the practical, as it has been for much of this book: final filings, creditor communications, team offboarding, and winding down operations, sometimes this can take months of some kind of busyness that fills the days.

These steps, though critical, are largely external. They're about logistics. But the internal process- the one happening inside the founder- often unfolds quietly, and long after the business has officially ended.

The truth is, business closure is not just a professional event; it's an emotional rupture. It challenges your identity, self-esteem, and sense of purpose. This is especially true for small business owners, where the line between personal and professional life is not just blurred- it's nonexistent. For many, the business was more than a job. It was a dream, a legacy, a vehicle for expression, freedom, impact. To close it feels like giving up a part of yourself and so often it has become our identity, what we are known for - what we are plastered all over LinkedIn with.

Some founders experience a deep sense of loss almost immediately. For others, including me, the grief is delayed, creeping in weeks or months after the fact.
It can show up as sadness, yes- but also as anger, guilt, numbness, and a pervasive sense of failure. The emotional terrain is complex, often cyclical, and rarely linear.

One founder I spoke to described it as "a low-level heartbreak I couldn't explain to anyone. I felt silly for being so upset about a business, but it had been my everything. Every decision I made for years came back to it."

I could really relate to that one.

The Loss of Identity
Perhaps one of the most destabilising aspects of business closure is the loss of identity. We live in a culture that often defines people by what they do. For founders, that's even more amplified.

You don't just work at a company - you are the company. Your name is on the website. Your face is on the social posts. Your story is baked into the brand narrative. When that ends, the question becomes: who am I now?

This identity crisis can manifest in surprisingly mundane ways. Updating your LinkedIn profile feels like an act of betrayal. Explaining "what you do" at a dinner party becomes awkward. You hesitate when writing emails from a personal account, no longer sure what your signature should say. These moments are small but deeply symbolic. They signal the end of something you poured your soul into- and the beginning of an uncertain chapter that hasn't been written yet.

It's tempting to rush through this discomfort. Many founders throw themselves immediately into the next thing - another business, a consultancy, a job. And while there's nothing wrong with moving forward, doing so without processing the emotional fallout can lead to repeating the same burnout, disconnection, or self-worth entanglement in the new venture.

Navigating Shame, Guilt, and Grief

There's a unique shame that comes with business failure - especially in a society that lionises entrepreneurship as the ultimate form of success. We idolise the bootstrapped founder who scaled to millions. We cheer for the startup that raised funding. But we rarely talk about the founders who quietly close their doors, who walk away without fanfare, who choose to stop not because they're weak- but because it's no longer right.

The result is that many founders internalise failure. They believe they weren't good enough, smart enough, or strong enough to make it work. They replay decisions in their mind like a courtroom cross-examination: Should I have launched earlier?

Was my pricing off? Did I ignore a red flag? The guilt becomes a soundtrack, and the shame can lead to withdrawal from peers, social media, or even family.

It's important to say this clearly: closing a business does not make you a failure. Businesses fail for many reasons- market shifts, timing, funding issues, health challenges, personal circumstances, economic downturns. Sometimes, the model doesn't scale. Sometimes, the founder outgrows the mission. Sometimes, things just don't work. That doesn't erase the value of the work you did or the courage it took to build something from nothing.

Understanding the Stages of Grief in Business Loss

Grief isn't just reserved for losing people. It shows up whenever we lose something that mattered deeply - an identity, a dream, a purpose. Grieving the loss of a business is not a weakness - it's a sign that you cared.

And when a business closes, that grief can move through you in waves. Unexpected ones. Illogical ones. And, at times, overwhelming ones.

While everyone experiences grief differently, it can be helpful to understand the five stages described by psychiatrist Elisabeth Kübler-Ross. Not because they form one of my neat little checklists- but because recognising them can help you feel less lost, less alone, and far less "crazy" for feeling the way you do.

1. Denial: "It's not really over."

This is the voice that says: *Maybe I can pivot. Maybe if I rebrand. Maybe if I just hang on a bit longer...*

Also known as frantically Googling 'Can I sell my company back to myself?' at 3am. Even after you've started the process of closure, denial can sneak in. It's not weakness- it's your brain protecting you from pain by trying to find another way out. You might find yourself checking the old website, refreshing analytics, or revisiting business plans late at night, imagining a comeback before you've even had a rest.

Denial isn't foolish. It's often a placeholder for pain that hasn't been fully felt yet.

2. Anger: "Why did this happen to me?"

The anger stage is loud- and often deeply private. It may be aimed at circumstances: *Why did the market crash? Why didn't my investors back me?* Or inward: *Why didn't I listen to my gut sooner? Why didn't I stop pouring money into something that wasn't working?*

There's anger at the unfairness. Anger at the missed signs. Anger at yourself, sometimes. Let it come. Let it move through you. Anger is often just hurt with its fists up.

3. Bargaining: "Maybe I can still save it..."

This is the mental loop of *what ifs* and *if onlys*. It's where you replay decisions over and over, trying to rewrite the past: *If I'd hired differently... If I'd launched earlier... If I'd raised more money...*

This stage can keep you stuck in rumination. But it's also a sign that you're searching for meaning - trying to make sense of what happened. That search can, eventually, lead you somewhere more stable.

4. Depression: "I don't know who I am without it."

This one's heavy. It's the dull ache that comes after the busyness fades. When there are no more deadlines, no more Slack messages, no more fires to put out- and you're left with the silence.

You may feel like you failed. Like no one's watching anymore. Like you've disappeared.

This sadness isn't weakness. It's love for what you built. It's your body and soul catching up with everything you've been carrying.

5. Acceptance: "It's over. And I'm okay."

This doesn't always arrive with fireworks. Sometimes, it's a quiet moment- when you close your laptop and no longer feel a pang of loss. When someone asks what you do, and you answer without a lump in your throat. When you look at your journey and feel... peace.

Acceptance doesn't mean you don't still miss it. It means you've made space for what comes next.

The fact is that your business was where you learnt how to run a business and when you realise that, and what a gift it has been you might be ready to move forwards again.

What Healing Actually Looks Like

Healing from a business closure is not a single moment of closure or clarity. It's a series of quiet steps, taken over time, often without a clear roadmap.

It might begin with rest - real rest, the kind where you don't check email or feel guilty about doing nothing. It might involve therapy or coaching, not to "fix" you, but to help you process what happened and reclaim a sense of self that isn't tied to output or achievement.

Many founders find it helpful to write out the story of the business - not the polished version, but the honest one. What were the highs? The lessons? The regrets? The turning points? What did you learn about yourself? This act of reflection, even if no one else ever reads it, can be incredibly powerful. It allows you to make meaning from the experience, rather than seeing it as a void.

Others create rituals to mark the end - a final blog post, a farewell letter to customers, a toast with friends. These symbolic acts help you close the loop, especially if the closure itself was sudden or messy.And perhaps most importantly, healing requires permission. Permission to feel proud. Permission to miss it. Permission to start again slowly. Permission to not rush into reinvention until you're ready.

Rebuilding Without Rushing

There's often pressure - internal and external - to move on quickly. People ask, "So what's next?" as if a timeline is required. But rebuilding after business closure isn't just about starting something new. It's about remembering who you are beyond what you built.

That may look like rest. Or travel. Or getting a job with a payslip for the first time in years. It may look like exploring new ideas slowly, without the urgency to monetise. It may involve healing your relationship with money, ambition, or control.

Some founders find their way back to business later- with clearer boundaries, deeper wisdom, and a renewed sense of purpose. Others find fulfilment in entirely different paths.

There is no correct route. The only wrong step is denying yourself the chance to pause and feel what needs to be felt.

You are not behind. You are not broken. You are simply in the in-between - the sacred, often messy space where transformation begins.

What You Keep

When a business ends, it's easy to feel like you've lost everything. But that's never the full story.

You keep your knowledge. Your skills. Your resilience. Your creativity. The relationships you built. The reputation you earned. The lessons - sometimes hard-won - that no course or mentor could have given you.

You keep your story. And in time, that story will not just be about what ended - but about what began after the ending.

Final Thought: There Is Life After Loss

In the wake of closure, you may feel invisible, I know I did. I'd had a national profile as a female tech founder - where did I go with that when I no longer had a tech start up - in fact, when I had a tech startup implosion. The spotlight moved. The messages stopped. The inbox is quiet. But your value has not disappeared.

When I stuck my head over the parapet, after two years away from the spotlight in a corporate role that wasn't even with a UK company, I was shocked at how quickly my network, reputation and profile resurrected themselves.

The end of a business is not the end of your impact. It is not the end of your capacity to create, connect, or contribute.

It is, quite possibly, the beginning of your most honest, liberated, and aligned chapter yet.

So take your time. Honour what you built. Mourn what was lost. And trust - truly - that your story isn't over.

"Grief is not a sign you failed. It's a sign that you loved something deeply. Let it move through you. Let it remind you that you are alive - and that there is still more ahead."

Interlude - What They Wish You Knew......

Building true resilience for yourself - not just your business

Contributed by Jayne Lewis, a leadership coach and Organisational Development practitioner whose expertise helps clients balance both potential and wellbeing.

When you lose the business that you've grown, many feelings emerge, including feelings of shame, failure, guilt, and grief. The most important advice I can give is - don't fight the feelings! It is important to sit with whatever comes, allow the grief to be felt – it's real grief for what you created and your dreams for the future.

Notice the emotions and name them. Where do you feel them? What's the story that they're telling you? These feelings aren't a sign that you are broken, they are natural and an important part of the healing process, the process that will enable you to move forward authentically and build true resilience.

Resilience is often seen as a way to avoid burnout or breakdown – a cycle of coping and bouncing back. True resilience is a measure of how much change we can adapt to successfully, our ability to reshape. Coping and bouncing back both come from a deficit way of thinking.

 - Coping is about not breaking down. If coping strategies are successfully stopping a breakdown, then coping is a great place to be, but it's inherently rigid.

Coping is a state where we need to control as much as possible to give us stability. Many coping strategies can be inherently unhealthy, whether that's excessive exercise, drinking, working long hours etc.

 - Bounce-back is about recovery from setback or trauma, and again bounce - back is great if the alternative is to be stuck in coping. But it involves riding the highs and lows of life and being in bounce-back can be fragile and we can slip back to coping.

True resilience isn't based on deficit thinking. Here you're resourceful, adaptable and energised. This is when resilience is about the ability to reshape, to thrive no matter what life throws up or stresses emerge.

The key to becoming truly resilient and finding a balance between your work and life, is to really know and understand yourself. As you move forward and find the next step that's right for you - whether this is starting a new business, moving into employment or a period of learning - my advice is to take time to reflect, and not rush into making a quick decision because certainty feels like a more comfortable place to be. Take the time to understand what brings you joy and fulfils you.

 To really know yourself you need to be willing to feel and recognise your emotions, and the stories you tell yourself when you feel a certain way. This is key to building true resilience. As you understand yourself better you will spot the signs that you maybe missed before.

 When you experience a particular situation, like the loss of a business, you will have three very different stories - with their own qualities – running in your mind.

The story we believe to be true will be related to the most active part of our nervous system at that time.

The situation is the same, but the stories are quite different:

1) Stories that emerge when your fight/flight system is activated, will have a flavour of danger and anxiety, as they come from a survival state.

2) When the story is rooted in the part of your nervous system linked to freeze/fawn, it will have an element of hopelessness or giving up.

3) There is always a third story, even if we can't hear it easily – this story is anchored in your regulated nervous system. This story will have a flavour of hope and possibility.

In any situation, each of these stories exists. If you're telling yourself a story from a state of fight or flight, stop and consider what the alternative stories are – I would write them down. Notice your feelings, where they are in your body, and what the story is that you're telling yourself. Now think about this from a place of regulation, what is the story here?

It can be hard in the moment, especially when things feel tough, but there is always a story of possibility running alongside the survival stories. Developing a habit where you're able to reflect on the three stories that are possible, and looking from a state of regulation takes practice but is a really good habit to develop.

Like all habits, this takes effort and practice, but the benefits are worth it. Understanding yourself and choosing your own story will enable you to make clearer decisions, and cope with the stresses that life brings.

Take the time to pause, process and rebuild at the pace that works for you. Ask for support and help from trusted friends and colleagues, or engage the support of a coach.

Working with a coach can help you to work through this process and stick to the decisions that you make, enabling you to build your resilience and spot early the signs that you may be slipping into a cycle of coping and bouncing back, or be in danger of burning out.

Chapter 13

From Ashes to Action - Lessons, Pivots & Restarting Smarter

From Endings, New Clarity

Every founder who has navigated the fire of business closure - whether dramatic or quietly executed - knows that something happens on the other side of it. At first, it's simply space: the silence where deadlines used to be, the time that was once filled with admin and pressure, the new ability to breathe without constant decision-making. But gradually, from that space, something else emerges too.

Clarity.

Not the kind that hits you like lightning, but the kind that builds slowly, quietly, like dew settling on a window. You begin to see the past differently. You start to piece together what was really going on beneath the surface. You begin to understand what you want moving forward - what you'll never compromise on again, and what you'll do better with the benefit of hindsight.

This final chapter is about that part of the journey. It's not about recovery - it's about renewal. It's about taking everything the experience of building, breaking, closing, and grieving has taught you, and shaping what comes next with purpose and wisdom.

Lessons That Only Failure Teaches

There are some lessons you simply can't learn through success. When things go well, you tend to keep moving, riding the momentum. It's in the slowing down - or the stopping altogether - that insight shows up. That's the strange gift of failure: it makes you pause. It makes you listen. It makes you reflect.

Many founders report that the most profound lessons came after things went wrong. Not just about cash flow or hiring or marketing - though those are real. But about themselves. About how much they'd tied their identity to performance. About how often they ignored their intuition.

How the lack of support they had as a child meant an over reliance on others, or the polar opposite, no support and a desire to prove things meant a fantastic lone ranger drama played out in the business. Not feeling good enough and constantly trying to prove they were. About how long they just stayed quiet when something felt off.

One founder said, "It wasn't until I closed the business that I realised I'd built it on someone else's definition of success. The whole thing was exhausting because it was never really mine."

These are not insights that show up in spreadsheets. They emerge in silence, in reflection, and in the courage to sit with discomfort long enough to ask what really matters.

Redefining Success on Your Terms

After closure, one of the most liberating - and disorienting - questions you'll face is: What does success mean to me now?

You get to choose. Perhaps for the first time, without the noise of outside expectations or metrics that never fit your life in the first place.

Success might no longer mean scaling fast or turning over six figures. It might look like:

- Building a business that supports your wellbeing

- Working with fewer clients, but more joy
- Making enough - and not needing to grow endlessly
- Having the freedom to take breaks without guilt
- Creating space for family, rest, or creativity

The point is: the definition is yours now. And once you've experienced what happens when a business overtakes your life, you're much less likely to make that mistake again.

The Reinvention Hangover - When "Better" Becomes a Burden

There's an odd pressure that sometimes sneaks in after the dust settles: the compulsion to come back swinging. To be shinier, wiser, faster. You feel like the next thing has to be flawless - like the only acceptable redemption arc is building a business so smooth, so strategic, so airtight that no one would ever guess what came before.

It's understandable. Failure - even quiet, thoughtful, intentional failure - can feel exposing. So we try to outrun it. We wrap our wounds in productivity. We rebrand before we've exhaled. We set up new systems and roadmaps and LinkedIn headers. We try to prove, mostly to ourselves, that this time, we're *better*.

But reinvention doesn't need to be a performance. Growth isn't a rush job. It's not your job to be impressive - it's your job to be *well*.

So if you feel like you should already be halfway into a new venture, but instead you're still taking naps and watching reruns and googling "low effort dinners," that's okay. You don't need a five-year plan yet. You don't need to be a phoenix. You're allowed to be a person.

Take your time. Your next thing doesn't need to be perfect. It just needs to be real.

How to Talk About Failure When You're Back in the Room

If you're a founder returning to employment - whether for stability, sanity, or simply a reset - one of the hardest parts can be explaining what happened. There's often a voice in your head whispering, *"They're going to think I'm a failure."* Or worse, *"They'll wonder what's wrong with me."*

Let's rewrite that inner script.

You didn't fail. You led. You built. You learned. You did more in a few years than most people attempt in a decade. And just because the outcome wasn't forever doesn't mean it wasn't valuable - or valued.

Here's the truth: most employers (and investors, and collaborators) aren't looking for perfection. They're looking for someone who knows how to solve real problems. Who can adapt. Who can lead with perspective. And nothing teaches those things faster than building something from scratch and seeing where it cracks.

Here's how to talk about it without flinching:

- "I ran a startup for [X years], and while we ultimately closed the business, I walked away with more commercial insight and leadership experience than I ever got in my early career."
- "I led a product and team through real-world market testing. We learned fast, adapted quickly - and I now know how to spot the red flags early."

- "I made decisions with incomplete data, wore twelve hats at once, and got very good at making things work under pressure. I'm bringing all of that with me."

And in networking conversations, you can soften the edges while still owning the story:

- "I built a business that taught me everything - including when to call time."
- "I've just wrapped up a chapter as a founder. Lots of learning, a few bruises, and a real appetite to work with people who value resilience."

The goal isn't to pretend nothing went wrong. It's to show that you're someone who can carry complexity, stay honest, and move forward - which, frankly, is the skillset of the future.

Because here's the thing most people won't say out loud: **those who've weathered failure often make the best hires, partners, and co-founders.** They've had their ego sanded down. They listen better. They know what actually matters.

And if the right person's across the table, they'll see that in you. But only if *you* see it in yourself first.

Spotting the Patterns- So You Don't Repeat Them

As you reflect, certain patterns often emerge.

Perhaps you ignored red flags because you didn't trust yourself. Perhaps you overworked because you tied your worth to output. Maybe you overextended financially because you were chasing a version of legitimacy. Or maybe you kept people around too long out of fear or loyalty.

These aren't failures of character. They're reflections of how deeply human we are. And when you name the pattern, you disarm its power. You become more aware the next time it shows up.

Restarting smarter isn't about eliminating all risk. It's about making better choices, earlier, with clearer eyes.

"The second time I built a business, I did it my way. I stayed small on purpose. I designed everything around my life. And it worked - not because it was bigger, but because it was truer."

Signs You're Ready to Rebuild

Not everyone returns to business right away. Some don't at all. But for those who do, there's often a moment when something clicks. Not a rush of adrenaline - but a gentle pull. An idea that sparks curiosity. A conversation that reignites a long-dormant skill. A sense of energy when thinking about what's possible.

You'll know you're ready when:
- You feel energised by creation, not pressured by urgency
- You can look back on your past business with perspective, not pain
- You want to build again - not to prove anything, but because it excites you

Restarting isn't about reclaiming old glory. It's about beginning from a new place, informed by experience, grounded in truth.

The Quiet Gift of Clarity

One of the most underrated parts of recovery is the clarity that sneaks in - not as a grand epiphany, but as quiet conviction.

It's in the moment you walk away from an opportunity that doesn't align. The gentle *no thank you* where there used to be a panicked *yes*. The sigh of relief when you realise you no longer feel the need to justify your slower pace, or your smaller goals, or your different path.

Clarity doesn't always arrive as a thunderclap. Sometimes it's in the way you protect your mornings now. Or the new ease you feel when you speak up in a meeting. Or the way you catch yourself before overcommitting.

You're not just rebuilding a business. You're rebuilding *self-trust*.

These small moments, these inner shifts, don't get celebrated like launches or revenue milestones. But they're the foundation of everything that comes next. You know what matters now. You know what you're not willing to lose again. And that knowing changes how you show up in every decision.

So when the world asks, *What's next?* remember: what's next doesn't have to be louder or bigger.

Sometimes what's next is simply more *you*.

Starting Over, but Not from Scratch

When you do decide to build again, you are not starting from scratch. You are starting from wisdom.

You know what to look out for. You understand your limits and boundaries.

You've seen what happens when the red flags are ignored. You've learned the value of sustainability, of rest, of asking for help early.

Entrepreneurs have an innate ability to go back to zero, to know the start intimately as something they are not afraid of. They know that you have to keep checking backwards, in order to move forward. That remembering your roots and why you started matters. They also intimately know the process needed to get to the end of a business

Whether your current or last business is a success or not, that is your education. You have a head start.

So just start. Take advantage of your knowledge and today's incredible tech, AI in particular.

Don't underestimate how valuable your ability to start from zero, again and again is.

Because in the days of AI you are the only person who limits your capability, if you are at this messy make or break point of running a business, you have more experience in business than most people graduating from top business courses.

In today's world there are three key things you need to think about if you want to make your business succeed:
1) How can you build an audience - what do you know deeply, what are you passionate about?
2) How can you use AI to engage the audience
3) What pricing model do you need to get the audience to pay

Skills in business are an asset, your audience is an asset, your reputation is an asset, assets are what will help you move forward.

Your new version of a business, if there is one, might look different. It might be smaller, slower, quieter. Or maybe it'll be bolder, freer, more unapologetic. Either way, it'll be yours.

And this time, you'll build with eyes open.

Designing the Life You Actually Want

Before you build the next thing, pause. Not to plot out the product or draft the business model- but to sketch out the *life* you actually want to live.

What do your ideal mornings look like? What pace feels sustainable? How much time do you want for creativity, rest, people you love? What are you no longer willing to sacrifice?

Most of us built our first business by accident. Not the business idea- that might have been intentional. But the shape of it. The hours. The habits. The chaos. We bolted systems onto dreams and tried to keep up.

This time, you get to flip the blueprint.

Start with your life. The rhythm of it. The needs of your body, your energy, your relationships. Then, if you still want to build something new, do it in a way that fits into that life, not one that consumes it.

Maybe that means setting caps on client hours. Maybe it means not monetising your next idea at all (what a rebellious thought). Maybe it means putting joy at the centre and letting everything else orbit around it.

Whatever it looks like, make sure it fits *you* first.

The business can follow.

Turning the Page, Not Erasing the Chapter

One of the most important things to remember is that the business you closed is not something to be hidden or buried. It's not a skeleton in the closet. It's a chapter. And often, it's one of the most powerful ones.

It's the story you'll tell to clients, collaborators, or investors. It's the experience that gives depth to your work. It's the credibility that comes not from theory, but from living through something real and hard.

You don't have to pretend it didn't happen. You get to own it. And in doing so, you show others what's possible after loss .I used to be ashamed of my first business closing.
Now (after several more closures) it's the story that connects me with the people I help. They trust me because I've been there.

Supporting Others Through What You've Lived

Your experience has value far beyond your next business.

Whether you choose to become a mentor, advisor, writer, speaker, or simply a peer who listens well, there is immense power in having been there.

As my friends and peers demonstrate, in their shares for this book and the conversations that helped me shape the content - so many of them had actually been there and I HAD NO IDEA!

Founders who've faced failure and come through it bring empathy, clarity, and honesty to the conversation in a way that no textbook ever could.

You understand what it feels like to cry over a missed payment. To lie awake calculating survival. To hold back tears in a team meeting. To walk away with dignity, even when the world wasn't watching.

You get to become the person you needed during your toughest moment.

And in doing so, you help others write better endings - and stronger beginnings.

The End That Was Never Really the End

We often talk about closure as a finality. But in business, and in life, it's rarely so neat.

Closure creates space. But it doesn't define you. You do.

This final chapter is a reminder that you are allowed to begin again. That the business you closed didn't waste your time, it prepared you. That failure isn't the opposite of success, it's part of it. That from ashes, something new can grow. Something wiser. Something kinder. Something more aligned.

This isn't just about restarting a business. It's about restarting yourself, with more truth, more courage, and more care than ever before.

Interlude: What They Wish You Knew... A Veteran Adviser on the Real Red Flags

Contributed by Warwick Hill, a trusted adviser to over 200 startups, whose counsel has shaped founders, saved companies, and occasionally stood beside them as they shut their doors with dignity.

On product-market fit and the danger of denial

"Product market fit is always a challenging topic with founders. They believe their idea or product can disrupt the market to carve a segment for themselves. I've seen this all too many times in failing companies. Founders should absolutely push boundaries and believe in their products - but it has to be tempered with practical, industry-led focus. I've watched people try to bend the market to their will and lose. It's OK to pivot when things aren't quite right. But to plough on regardless of industry feedback is both emotionally reckless and unfair to staff, investors, and everyone else involved. A red flag? When a founder insists the product must be exactly as they've imagined it, and won't course-correct despite mounting evidence."

On seeking help too late — and the consequences

"A serial entrepreneur once asked me to help raise a Series A investment. But the company's positioning was wrong. As I began reshaping the investment narrative, I discovered the financials weren't accurate. Whether the founder was misleading others deliberately or not wasn't for me to say - but we had two months of runway left. What began as a funding round turned into a rescue mission and then into a distressed asset sale. Why? Because the founder got distracted by the next shiny thing in Silicon Valley and refused to back a business loan he'd guaranteed. Prior success doesn't guarantee future outcomes, no matter how many VCs want to believe it. Coming late and being dishonest? That was always going to backfire."

On closing with dignity

"I advised a business that delivered analytics to the restaurant industry. They were scaling steadily - sales were solid, the tech team were building features. Then came Covid. The whole sector collapsed. We couldn't save the company. But I set aside unpaid invoices and supported the founders as they made the tough calls - with compassion. They spoke openly and truthfully with staff, suppliers, and advisors. People rallied behind them because it wasn't about blame; it was about being human in the face of something no one could control."

On the common blind spots: regulation and margin

"Regulatory blind spots are everywhere - in startups and big corporations alike. Founders need to know how their product interacts with data laws and compliance frameworks. Ignore that and you're front-page news for all the wrong reasons. Financially, the biggest flaw I see is a lack of margin analysis. Founders chase runway and freebies to stay afloat, but forget that without understanding margin, there's no scale. Investors won't touch a business with weak margins. Post-seed and into Series A, a founder has to become an executive. They must understand the building blocks - costs, ROI, margin. Those who do? They succeed. Those who don't? They fail."

On burnout - the shadow that follows

"Founder burnout is like a shadow - always there, rarely recognised. I've been through it twice. The loneliness, the emotional grind, the constant repetition - it wears you down. You push through long days, skip holidays, and the people closest to you pay the price. Every great entrepreneur I know has a long-suffering partner behind them - they're the heroes, the emotional regulators. When founders burn out, they lose focus, perspective, and objectivity. Emotions distort decision-making. That's why VCs favour teams who can manage the emotional turbulence. If you can't regulate yourself, it spills out into the business and drags it down."

On honesty, and when to share (or not)

"We talk about transparency in business all the time - but for founders, it's a double-edged sword. Telling your board or investors you're burnt out might be honest, but it often triggers a wave of risk-mitigation behaviour you can't undo. That's why I always say: every founder needs a support hero. Someone they can talk to without fear of repercussion. You can't disclose vulnerability to your team, and you can't always share frailty with the board. Oversharing has consequences. Dishonesty, though, is worse - especially in regulated industries, where the penalties are severe. Walk the line. Be honest, but strategic."

On the worst kind of advisers

"Opinions are like arseholes - everyone has one. There are far too many so-called advisers recycling ancient wisdom for equity. Let me be blunt: giving equity to an adviser who pops in for four weeks of ideas? That's just wrong. Would you give your accountant equity? No. So why give it to some random adviser? I've advised 200+ startups and I've never taken equity. Two reasons: (1) I wouldn't respect myself, and (2) it creates conflicts of interest. My mantra? Pay my invoice and use me like a hired gun. I'll give you the best advice I've got - no agenda, no strings."

On failure and the fear of it

"Failure isn't the problem - the fear of failure is. It causes more damage than the failure itself. When a business goes under, I help founders with the practical stuff - and the emotional load. You've got to protect staff, manage the fallout with suppliers and investors, and most of all, avoid turning it into a personal shame spiral. We learn more from failure than success. Take the loss, yes - but take the lessons too. Emotional growth, better people skills, smarter margins, clearer product thinking - whatever it is, take something from the fire and turn it into fuel."

Final advice for founders asking for help
"Have a clear ask. Don't expect it to be free - good advice costs. Do your research. Be concise. Protect your IP. Know when to walk away from a bad adviser. Founders who flourish are the ones who know how to ask for help - and when."

Conclusion: It Ain't Over Til...

There's a moment in every founder's journey- sometimes in year one, sometimes after a decade, when things start to wobble. When certainty begins to slip. When what once felt exciting and expansive starts to feel uncertain, heavy, even unsustainable.

For some, that moment is brief and passes with the right decision or shift. For others, it stretches into months, or years, where quiet warning signs are ignored, support feels scarce, and the founder carries more weight than anyone realises.

This book was written for that moment.

- It's for the business owner in the moment where they are staring at the numbers at 2am, heart pounding.
- It's for the entrepreneur in the moment when they are trying to motivate a team while secretly feeling empty.
- It's for the visionary who is having a moment of feeling ashamed to admit that their plan isn't working.
- It's for the founder who quietly closed the doors and for the moment hasn't told anyone why.
- It's for the person who once loved their business, and now just wants a moment to breathe.

What you've read isn't just a manual. It's a mirror. It's a map. It's a reminder that what you're experiencing is normal. That you're not broken, or failing, or behind. That recognising problems, asking for help, making hard decisions, closing, pivoting, or starting again - these aren't signs of weakness.

They're signs of leadership. Real leadership.

The kind that isn't always celebrated in headlines or LinkedIn wins.

The kind that happens in kitchens, co-working spaces, late-night journal entries, difficult conversations, and long walks alone.

The kind that says: I want to build something better, and I want to be well while doing it.

Throughout these chapters, we've looked at the many reasons a business might struggle or stop- from financial chaos and market shifts to personal burnout, investor pressure, and toxic team dynamics. We've unpacked what it means to let go, how to honour endings, and how to find yourself again in the silence that follows.

But most of all, we've made space for the truth: that business is personal.

It touches every part of your life. It shapes your identity, your relationships, your self-worth. So when something breaks, of course it hurts. Of course you grieve. Of course you question everything. And that's okay. That's human.

If I had to distill the messages I want you to take from this book, it's here:

You get to keep going.
You get to rebuild differently.
You get to rest without apology.
You get to speak honestly about the hard parts.
You get to learn from what happened - not be defined by it.
You get to start again, on your terms, in your time.

Your choice.

Because it ain't over til...

You say it's over.

Or until it becomes something new.

This book doesn't promise easy answers. But it offers something more important: companionship through the hard parts, and tools to help you navigate them.

Whether you're trying to turn things around, choosing to close, or planning your return, I hope this book has given you the language, support, and strength to do it all with honesty and grace.

Your story isn't over.

And when you're ready - I'll be here, as will all my colleagues, peers, advisers and friends who contributed to this book and in their own way have cheered me on. We'll be cheering you on as you write the next chapter.

Your next chapter.

(so go on then what are you waiting for?!)

The Beginning...

About the Author

Jo Eckersley is an award-winning entrepreneur, author, and strategic advisor who has spent more than three decades helping founders and small businesses navigate growth, innovation, and recovery. As the founder of Finitie - a consultancy that supports founders to be more efficient across their business and a digital platform that connects startups with fractional experts when they need it - she brings a rare blend of lived experience, technical understanding, and deep empathy for the challenges of building a business in turbulent times.

A former award-winning tech founder who rebuilt after burnout and business closure, Jo has transformed that experience into practical guidance for others. Through her work with Innovate UK as an Assessor and Monitoring Officer, her mentoring sessions with various business support and charitable organisations, and her consultancy work across the creative industries, she has supported thousands of innovation projects across the UK's creative, digital, and innovation sectors, championing sustainable start-up growth and founder wellbeing.

Jo's writing and speaking centre on the human side of entrepreneurship - the resilience, reinvention, and real-world recovery that rarely make the headlines. It Ain't Over 'Til... is her first book, written for every founder who's had to start again, and a reminder that failure isn't final - it's feedback.

She lives in Buckinghamshire, with her daughter and toddler grandson, continues to advise early-stage companies, leads Marketing, Business and AI-focused workshops, and is building a community of founders committed to doing business better.